As an international entrep... alike worldwide. We have similar needs and share the potential to be hacked both personally and professionally. The authors of *Unhackable Force* have beautifully broken down what it takes to reset and reclaim this story called life. This is a must-read for women realizing we are stronger locally and globally by uniting through mutual respect, compassion, understanding, truth, and vision.

—Rosalyn Fremder, Owner and Director at Expat Help, Netherlands, UK, Host of *House Hunters International* HGTV, featured on *PBS* television and in *Fortune Magazine* and *The New York Times.*

I know what it's like to get hacked. I also know what it's like to surround yourself with others striving for a better future. *Unhackable Force* is about recovering and reclaiming the gifts and power within you to live the life you are created for. With practical steps, faith, and effort, you can become the winner God created you to be. *Unhackable Force* will get you back on track.

—Sonya Jones
Author, Motivator, Speaker, and
Season 16's *Biggest Loser* Finalist
Owner of Losin' It with Sonya Jones Weight Loss Clinic

There is nothing better than women coming together to encourage, uplift, and inspire each other. As the authors said in this book, *"Individually we may be fierce, but together we become a force."* That's exactly what you will learn during the 30-day journey. I loved every second of it. I highly recommend this book to any woman who is ready to go to her next level in life. This book will help propel you to do just that!

—Sonya Fernandez
Author and Health Coach

I've worked with Niccie for years, seeing how passionate she is about sharing "The Good News" to transform homes, communities, and ultimately the nation. The *Unhackable Force* book and program powerfully reaches the masses as Niccie, Debra Hayes, Daphne V. Smith, and Lisa Moser connect with women in all areas of their faith and life, helping them wipe out the footholds that overwhelm the world and try to hack us.

—Shemane Nugent
Lifestyle and Healthy Living Expert,
*New York Times* Bestselling Author

# Unhackable Force

## Closing the Gap to Reset, Redo, and Reclaim a Life of Favor!

A 30-Day Journey to
Release Your Pain,
Receive Your Permission,
Rediscover Your Passion,
and Rock Your Purpose

Debra Lynn Hayes
Daphne V. Smith
Lisa Moser
Niccie Kliegl

Published by Unhackable Press
P.O. Bo 43, Powell, OH 43035

Scripture taken from NIV, NTE,, MSG, AMP, TPT, NLT, and NKJV
All rights reserved.

Paperback: 978-1-955164-03-0
Hardback: 978-1-955164-04-7
Ebook: 978-1-955164-05-4

Library of Congress Control Number: 2021925507

# Dedication

*This book is dedicated to all women.*
*By your very DNA, you are strong. You are fierce.*
*It's your time and your turn to become all you*
*are created to be. You are made for more.*

# CONTENTS

## PART 3: UNHACKABLE REACH

## PART 4: UNHACKABLE CALL

## Part 5: Unhackable Elevation

# FOREWORD

When Daphne V. Smith, Debra Lynn Hayes, Lisa Moser, and Niccie Kliegl decided to write *Unhackable Force*, I knew they were the perfect choice to expand upon my book, *Unhackable*. I want this message to reach the far ends of the earth, and these four women are the positive force for change to make that happen.

Women young and old will resonate with the Unhackable F.O.R.C.E message. I've had the deep honor of working with all four women. I've coached them, and I've seen them grow as leaders and communicators. Here's a sneak peek into what you can expect.

**F = Favor:** Debra will reach those with a message of hope and triumph over darkness and hard times. We can get hacked when life is hard, but circumstances don't have to define us. So, when disappointments, heartaches, and tragedies won't back down, Debra will show you how to unmask the hope inside and embrace a life of favor.

**O = Opportunity:** For years, I've seen Daphne coach clients out of opposition and into opportunity. She is a powerhouse with her clients. If you feel like your life circumstances have gotten you in a corner, she will kick down the walls and usher you through to your next best step.

**R = Reach:** For years, Lisa has been helping others reach their full potential. Whether on stage or in her personal life, Lisa is passionate about assisting others in getting clear, confident, and connected for purpose-driven life and service. If you feel misdirected or unclear on who you are or how you are designed to connect with others, Lisa will get you there.

**C = Call:** Niccie is all about the call God has on your life. If you feel hacked, wondering where the abundance is that so many talk about or others have, Niccie will show you. I've worked with Niccie for years, and she will not let you go until you are in your sweet spot, tapping into all the Trinity offers, and taking you farther than you ever dreamed possible.

**E = Elevate:** By banding together, these ladies know *all* women can become a powerful force in their work and life. The *Unhackable F.O.R.C.E.* will show you how to unite and empower one another to reach far beyond the things you only dream of today.

Debra, Daphne, Lisa, and Niccie will help you rewrite your story called LIFE. Maybe you have been distracted, or perhaps you have a fear of leaving a comfort zone. Maybe your story involves tragic, life-changing events completely out of your control.

It is time to write a new story.
It is time to dream again.
What is stopping you?

—Kary Oberbrunner
CEO of Igniting Souls Publishing Agency
*Wall Street Journal* and *USA Today* best-selling author of *Unhackable*

# START HERE

Everyone not only has a story, but everyone *is* a story. Age, experience, location, background, vocation, or education has little bearing on these stories called *life*. Very few people would say their life is one not requiring resets, retakes, or redos.

Why is that? Why are the best-intended life stories often derailed or *hacked*? As small children, we dreamed. Our mind was an open playing field, and imagination was our best friend. There was no fear of changing directions. One day we were a princess or fireman, the next a nurse or a cowboy. No condemnation or self-limitations slowed our imagination. In our minds, we were off to the next adventure and capable of anything.

Teen years and young adulthood possibly opened our stories of self-doubt, poor self-image, bad decisions, bullying, and the like. Our dreams began getting hacked with limitations of thoughts. *What if I can't do it? What if they don't like me? What if I look foolish? What if I don't have enough?* Perhaps later in life, the story turned that page.

College and careers may have brought their own hacking of expectations. Maybe the world belonged to you until—until that promotion meant to be yours didn't go through, until unfulfilled promises broke you, or until that hard-earned degree didn't open the anticipated doors.

Let's stop a minute and look at this word we continue to use. *Hacked.* Hacking simply means someone or something gained unauthorized access to a system or computer. Although we often think of electronic devices getting hacked, humans become hacked as well. Our bodies are composed of *systems* (respiratory, circulatory, digestive, and immune, to name a few), and our brains operate like *supercomputers*. Navigating our noisy world long enough to accomplish our daily tasks—much less do our dreams—is nearly impossible, especially these days. The odds are clearly stacked against us, and temptations lurk less than an arm's length away. Think of all the things that hack your attention and time: smartphones, multitasking, social media, streaming videos, and advertisements, not to mention all the decisions we have to make daily. Thanks to advances in science and technology, the amount of information doubles every twelve hours.[1]

Hacking extends from the deceiving thoughts telling our stories to all the noise society makes as it clamors for our attention.

The authors of this book will show you how to rewrite your story called *life*. Maybe you have been distracted, have procrastinated, or have a fear of leaving a comfort zone. Perhaps your story may involve tragic life-changing events completely out of your control. It is time to write a new story. It is time to dream again. What is stopping you?

"Denying your old story is an exercise in futility. It feels inauthentic to ignore your personal history like you're trying to swallow a lie. So rather than attempting to forget your past, create the space for a new future instead. Use the words *up until now.*

These three words will allow you to change your story rather than regurgitating the old one subconsciously swimming in your head. In a way, it's a weapon to ward off the self-sabotaging thinking that hacked you in the past. *Up until now* gives you permission to write a new story instead. Think of it as your first act of co-creation, a legitimate effort to return to your childhood days. You'll sink your teeth into a simpler version of life once again."[2]

The authors—Debra Lynn Hayes, Daphne V. Smith, Lisa Moser, and Niccie Kliegl—each admit their life stories have been in the throes of being hacked.

**Debra** has faced divorce, financial ruin, and the unthinkable tragedies of burying four children. Through all her circumstances, she feels the greatest threat of being hacked was the quilt she lived under, resulting from a bad decision.

Was God punishing her by allowing pain into her life that was completely out of her control?

**Daphne's** interrupted childhood, establishing and creating patterns for susceptibility to abuse, hacked her for decades until she began to understand who she really is outside her experiences and treatment from others.

**Lisa** has worn crowns from many beauty titles and looked like a confident, powerful woman, yet she struggled with stepping into that woman she portrayed. Being a huge people-pleaser and a professional at making sure people feel welcomed and accepted, she diluted her personality to match others' energy and make them feel comfortable. When she discovered the secret to stepping into her power and not shrinking to fit others, she tapped into her passion. "Passion is the game changer from feeling stuck to moving to the next stage of your life."

**Niccie** overcame a childhood learning disability, which created an overwhelming desire to inspire hope in others, help them believe in themselves so they can find the grit the world cannot provide. Niccie calls this *Tapping into the Trinity* and has built her coaching practice around it for both life and business.

Each author has been fierce in rewriting her story. Individually, they have proven change can and will happen with prayer, determination, intentional steps, guts, and strength.

They also realized rewriting a life story is a journey. As long as we are breathing, we will have those *up until now* moments.

Rewriting your story is not only changing direction from hurt and pain to peace and fulfillment; it's also going from good to better or better to great. We are called to excellence, and excellence is a journey. *Up until now* is a stepping-stone to discovering the hacks of your life, giving yourself permission to take control, finding your passion, and stepping into your purpose and calling.

By uniting together, the authors have elevated their individual ability to be fierce and become a *force*—not just any force, but an Unhackable Force. Debra, Daphne, Lisa, and Niccie will lead you on your path to becoming part of the Unhackable Force as well. They recognize that strong, mature individuals, such as yourself, become stronger and find greater purpose when they unite. The authors' goal is to empower others and be an example of what can happen when fierce women join together with mutual respect, encouragement, power, truth, and vision (and a lot of fun thrown in the mix).

*Force* is strength or energy exerted or brought to bear; cause of motion or change; moral or mental strength. The word *force* can often have a negative tone, seen as a manipulative power. In this book, the authors will reveal the true and positive life-changing definition behind being a force. Each letter of the word can be a page-turning experience as you rewrite your story.

**F—Favor**
**O—Opportunity**
**R—Reach**
**C—Call**
**E—Elevate**

Now to meet your authors!

**Debra** will guide you through Days 2–8 as your new story begins, with examining where you are today, what hacked you, and how to plow up the ground of past pain, plant seeds, and watch a newly designed life develop.

**Daphne** will walk with you during Days 9–15 as you learn to give yourself permission to take control, make the necessary changes, and find your courage.

**Lisa** is your example of passion. Spend Days 16–22 with her as your darkness becomes light and your purpose appears.

**Niccie** will bring clarity to your connection to your creator and community during Days 23–29 as you embrace your calling.

On Day 30, all the authors will check in with you to welcome you to the *force* as you elevate to your next steps. Your new story, new life, and vision will empower you to be the person who resonates with the core of your being. Your life of favor awaits you. Reset, redo, and reclaim it.

Before we begin your amazing journey, let's meet your guides and get to know more about their stories and connection to each other.

# Day 1
## WRITE YOUR STORY

*The best part about your story is that the next page is blank,
and you get to write it.*

—Chris Butler

## DEBRA

Hi! I'm Debra.

I am honored you are giving your time to embrace this book and unite with us. You will engage with each author, and I guarantee one of our stories will resonate with you. We each bring different perspectives and experiences, so somewhere among the four of us, you will find yourself.

I met Daphne, Lisa, and Niccie in 2015 when we were part of the same author coaching group. It didn't take long to recognize the depth, genuineness, compassion, fun, fire, and determination within these ladies. You will get to know each of us on a deeper level as you discover how characteristics of being unhackable can be found in anyone and under any circumstance.

I am from the South. I grew up in East Tennessee but have lived in several places stretching from Chicago to Florida. Currently, I live in St. Augustine, Florida, with my Amazon parrot, Jazz. She is quite hilarious and is gaining her own social media following.

Let me begin by saying that as I share my personal story, I do not think my pain has been more significant than the struggles of others. I do not put my tragedies on a pedestal or in print for pity. My goal is to show that regardless of circumstance, there is always a choice to walk in favor, become unhackable, and enjoy life to the fullest.

I wrote my book *RISE . . . What To Do When Hell Won't Back Off* to encourage others who have faced disappointment, heartache, or tragedy. Pain is unavoidable. It does not have to define our lives. I want to use my experiences of burying four children, divorce, and financial ruin to encourage you. No matter what has tripped you up in life, you can *rise* above it. You can take control. You can unmask the hope deep inside you and embrace the beautiful life you were intended to live.

My greatest hack came against my relationship with God. Even with a solid Christian foundation, I was angry and didn't want anything to do with God. The beauty of His faithfulness is he never turns his back on us, even when we feel like throwing in the towel. The book of Hebrews from the New Testament tells us to encourage one another while it is still today. That is my goal. I want to encourage you in your "today." You can't change your past and may not have tomorrow, but *today* is where you are. Today is within your control and is what matters.

My book *RISE* shares the details of my life, but let me lay the foundation of the story I had to rewrite.

My life began as one of perfection with two parents who loved me unconditionally. We were not the wealthiest family in town, but our home was rich with love. Loneliness was my constant companion as an only child. My early days of creating my own entertainment with imaginary playmates planted seeds of independence and strength to stand alone. Those were attributes I would need for the future awaiting me.

The first shocking experience happened at age fifteen, with the fatal accident of a dear friend. Processing death as a teenager quickly became a game of numbing pain that affected my decisions for years to come. I developed a deep-rooted fear of loss. Each time someone got close to my heart, I ran. That pattern led to three broken engagements.

After the engagements ended and before I met my future husband, I found myself pregnant. Fear of the future took a deep hold and led to the worst decision of my life. I had an abortion.

Not long afterward, I met a man with a nine-year-old son. I fell in love with this child. His mom had recently passed from cancer. Maybe he needed a mom. Perhaps I needed a child. Whatever the reason, I married his father. We had become great friends, but admittedly we should not have married when we did. He carried the fresh wound of losing his wife, and I carried the fresh wound of the abortion. We were two broken people numbing pain together. If we had taken time to heal, perhaps we wouldn't have married, or maybe the marriage would have been strong enough to survive the hurricane of tragedies ahead.

Three years into the marriage, I delivered a stillborn son. Within months, I gave birth to another son who lived an hour. Three years later, my nineteen-year-old stepson was killed in a work-related accident. Our world was rocked to the core. Divorce and financial ruin followed. My faith, already questionable, became nonexistent (or so I thought).

In *RISE,* I go into many details about my struggles and how God's grace and love chipped away at my deceptive thoughts to shine light into that dark mental world where I lived. My healing began the night I battled suicide. Some people question a Christian having suicidal thoughts. Thoughts are our greatest enemy and are no respecter of persons.

So yes, the battle was real. Having the choice to die or pray for help, I chose to pray. Yet, all I could get out of my mouth was, "God, I can't trust my husband, and I don't even like you." That was it. My honesty with myself and God is the place my true healing began.

As a former international corporate liaison, I strategized success for individuals and teams. Today, I use those same skills to empower others facing personal devastation.

Walk with me from Days 2-8. I will encourage you to identify what is being hacked in your life and the steps you can take to begin seeing the obstacles move. Together, we will take a deep dive into exactly what it means to live a life of favor.

## DAPHNE

Hi! I'm Daphne.

I have always loved learning. Growing up, I was the girl who loved reading, experimenting, and exploring. Was it something new? Let's try it! That sense of wonder and curiosity ultimately led me to the time on my journey when I met Deb, Lisa, and Niccie.

As Deb mentioned, we all met through an author coaching program. She left out, however, that thousands of people are part of that program. So how did the four of us connect? It started when I was at one of the lowest points of my life. In hindsight, what seemed like a valley was a pathway to a mountaintop.

In February 2014, I took one of the biggest and scariest risks of my life. I walked out on my unhealthy and highly dysfunctional marriage, which at the time was in its twenty-seventh year. I shocked myself as well as my now ex-husband when I finally decided enough was enough. Through that separation, I was introduced to opportunities that eventually led me to meet my co-authors a year later. Never doubt a detour. It could lead to an amazing and unexpected blessing.

The bond among the four of us was not instantaneous. All three of them intimidated me: Deb with her bold self-assurance, Lisa with her ability to relate to and connect with others effortlessly, and Niccie with her clear focus and "I can accomplish anything" mindset. They each had qualities I envied and admired. Thankfully, they each also had a heart larger than my home state of Texas, a Christ-centered spirit of grace, and an inclusive attitude.

The decades of abuse, brokenness, trauma, and shame I experienced during my marriage made me doubt I had anything to offer these dynamic women. I desperately wanted to associate with like-minded women. I searched in myriad places, from direct sales and vocational ministry to the fitness industry, trying to find my "tribe."

Even with all my seeking, I still couldn't find my people because I was unclear about who I truly was. Have you ever felt hungry and couldn't identify what would taste good or satisfy you? You don't know if salty and crunchy will hit the spot or if creamy and sweet will satisfy. Maybe some veggies and protein?

Yearning to satiate my hunger, void, and lack led me to search. I've learned a few lessons along the way. I will share some of them with you in this book, as I do when working with my coaching clients. One of the main concepts I want to share concerns giving yourself permission. When you allow yourself the possibility and opportunity to be creative and break through mental and emotional barriers, you open yourself to new levels of healing, hope, and wholeness.

We'll spend Days 9–15 together exploring and working on the ideas and application:

- **Resolve**—Trying harder isn't always the answer
- **Create**—Clearing our blocks to allow for new creation

- **Time**—Trusting your gut affects your timing
- **Space**—Surrounding yourself with chosen people and things
- **Urgency**—Deciding someday is not found on any calendar
- **Agency**—Maximizing your sense of priority
- **Energy**—Harnessing and focusing your power

During our time together, we're going to clear out some cobwebs as we work toward becoming an Unhackable Force—you know, those sticky things that feel yucky and cling to us almost invisibly? We're going to recognize roadblocks, whether self-imposed or determined by others. We're going to release ourselves to embrace our full potential, and we're going to reclaim the power we might have leaked out over the years by accepting false beliefs.

When the clearing happens, you'll be free to embrace what's been in you all along—your passion. Understanding that passion is Lisa's sweet spot. Once you get to her days, you'll be fresh and ready to explore and exude what you love and what the world needs.

Once you've gone through the pain and given yourself permission, you get to gather your passion for living your purpose.

We recognize ourselves as a force because we know that when power unites, paradigms shift. We've personally experienced it, and we want you to because you deserve it, and your call has not yet been fulfilled.

## LISA

Hi! I'm Lisa.

I couldn't be more excited to be a part of your journey. The women I have the privilege to write this book with have become some of my very best friends. They are truth-tellers and powerhouses! That being said, like you, we *all* have our stories.

At twenty-four, I stood on the Miss USA stage, looking like a confident young woman. I was called one of the fifty most beautiful women in the world that year. You would think I had it all together, right? I was a tall, thin, confident young woman who was so proud to be standing on that stage, but people didn't know that I didn't feel like I belonged there, and I wasn't the strong woman I appeared to be.

What was missing? I had not learned the power of passion and reach yet, but I was learning.

It took years of training to figure it all out, going about it on my own. I had no manual or personal guru coach, only a life of trial and error, learning through all my mistakes and *stuckness*, from reading tons of books, and from meeting great friends and mentors along the way.

How I got to that stage is a story in itself, and I don't want to spend a lot of time telling it. If you are interested, I wrote about it in my book *Miss Conception: 5 Steps to Overcome Our Misconceptions and Achieve Our Own Crowning Moment*. I shared how we all have misconceptions about ourselves and others that hold us back from our best lives and what we can do to overcome five major misconceptions that trip us up every time. It's an excellent book for women of all ages, and I *love* when mothers and daughters read it together. It gets such a great dialog going between them and promotes a better understanding of each other and how we all deal with things at every age.

I want to start with the lessons I began to understand after I returned home from Miss USA. After I met and married my husband, I once again found myself searching for that thing—that something to fulfill me again.

I am a goal setter by nature. I love setting my sights for something and then going for it! I have been a dreamer from a very young age, but aren't we all dreamers as kids? I bet you were, too.

When I was in grade school, I had mad leadership skills. Some may have called me bossy, but when I see bossy young girls, I see future leaders. I don't remember having low self-esteem, worrying about people not liking me, or feeling stuck when I was young. Nope, I was just being myself. What I was passionate about was playing make-believe, and I did it every chance I had.

As I got older, that make-believe turned to dreaming, goal setting, and the feeling I got once I accomplished something. This went on through high school, into my work, and into finding myself on the Miss USA stage.

One reason I didn't feel I belonged on that stage was my fear of public speaking. I never dreamed of becoming a public speaker in high school. If I had to stand in front of the room and give a book report or a speech, I would be sick to my stomach. But when I won the title of Miss Ohio USA, I was thrust into the speaking world. I had to make appearances and stand on stage and talk to people about a chosen topic. It was sink or swim, so I learned to tread water!

I wasn't confident at all and never thought I could win, but it was the training ground for my future, and I didn't even know it.

Fast forward to a husband, two little girls, and that unfulfilled, stuck feeling. I mean, come on! How can you feel dissatisfied and stuck when you have everything you could have ever dreamed of, right? I had a home, a beautiful family, and a job I loved, but it all felt like being on autopilot. When I allowed myself a minute or two to dream and set those goals, I told myself I wasn't smart enough, young enough, or didn't know enough—simply a whole lot of "not enough"—even to go beyond the little thought I dared to dream. Age and responsibility do that to us.

Have you ever felt like there's something you've always dreamed of doing or wanted to accomplish, but you didn't feel you were good enough, didn't have it in you, or simply didn't believe in yourself enough to try? Where do you even begin? I relate to this because it's happened to me many times in my life, as I'm sure it has you.

When we connect what we want to do with our passion, things happen, turn, and become a reality. That is what my heart is with my section of this book.

> **NEWS ALERT:** *I wasn't always a confident woman and still have my days—like everyone. It doesn't matter if you are a famous actor, supermodel, corporate powerhouse, a Miss USA contestant, or a woman trying to figure out what's next for her; we all suffer from imposter syndrome or lack of confidence sometime in our lives.*

Years later, I had a **passion** project I needed to share with the world! I returned to pageantry as a vehicle to get that message heard. I won the title of Mrs. Ohio and won the national title of Mrs. International, which afforded me many opportunities. I was privileged to:

- Become a national spokesperson for The American Diabetes Association.

- Publish a children's book.

- Work with an international pharmaceutical company.

- Become an educator and speaker for an international health and wellness company.

- Become a speaker for Nationwide Insurance.

- Television and radio work.

- Speak at and host events around the US.

I knew then that the pageant wins were for a much bigger reason than merely a crown and banner. I knew what I had learned about sharing one's voice, and its impact on people was something I needed to teach others. I didn't learn it all overnight; it has been a journey, but once you discover the joy in the journey, your life has a whole new perspective.

**My heart is to help others see the value in their voice, message, and passion and help them share it with the world to make the impact they know they can. I have a love for educating and encouraging others to understand and break free from the misconceptions that hold them hostage and keep them from stepping on the next *stage* in life.**

Let's journey together from Day sixteen through twenty-two and discover and unleash your superpower to step onto that next S.T.A.G.E.!

## Niccie

Hi! I'm Niccie.

I want to start by welcoming you to the final chapters of this book. It's the perfect place for me to work with you. I love *the final hour* and have powered through some amazing things at the last minute.

Those who know little about me quickly learn I have a strong passion for inspiring others to accomplish things they may feel are impossible. You are never too old, and it is never too late.

Where did this passion come from? My past, which had I allowed it, could have been onerous and prevented me from achieving. You see, I barely learned to read. Had our family not moved to a wonderful little town, I'm not sure I would have. At twelve years old, I could hardly get through a Dr.

Seuss book. My brilliant sister, eight years younger than I, read better than I did at twelve or thirteen. With a lot of grit and superb, patient, loving teachers who believed in me, I figured it out. I believe in you, too. I believe in everyone I work with.

There are a few key components to me learning to read, becoming the director of nursing for two nursing homes at age twenty-six, and starting an online business at forty-six—when I thought my husband and I would settle down for early retirement. I'll be sharing those elements with you in my portion of the book, Days 22–29:

- **Embodying** your divine mastery over worldly slavery

- **Engaging** your God-given makeup

- **Understanding** your good and bad triggers

- **Assessing** your growth for Sabbath-style excellence

- **Clarifying** your call by wisdom *over* knowledge

- **Crafting** your favor statement with God's script

- **Communicating** your favor to increase your faith and favor

I can't wait to break down these lessons with you and for you to begin your daily exercises. For now, I want you to know that these seven days will help you step into all you've been called to do.

For the better part of five years, I've been growing a faith-based life and business coaching practice. God has greatly blessed it. The work He has done and is doing on me, I am sharing with others in my book series, *The Legacy Series*. The books are designed to be your private coach in the comforts of your home. Book one, *The Living Legacy*, is all about getting your life deeply partnered with the Trinity and learning to tap into all God, Jesus, and the Holy Spirit offer. It's powerful.

Book two takes that relationship deeper with God as He asks you to share Him with your loved ones. The book's subtitle, *As For Me & My House*, references how to elevate the lives of those within your home by partnering with God as well.

Book three, *The Learning Legacy*, is coming out next spring and will take your faith further by going deeper with Jesus.

Book four is titled *The Leading Legacy*, teaching the reader to partner deeply with the Holy Spirit to transform our world.

It sounds a bit overwhelming, right? Well, I'm going about it one day at a time, often crunching in the final hour with God's great might and glory. I love showing others how to tap into the Trinity for power and might they didn't know they had.

No matter your past, age, size, shape, color, present, or future, you are called, and I want to help you learn of it and step in boldly.

# PART 1

## UNHACKABLE FAVOR

# DAY 2
## YOU ARE YOUR STORY

*Your life is your story. Write well. Edit often.*

—Unknown

Welcome back! I am excited to journey with you from Day 2-8 in this section called Unhackable Favor! You are probably asking yourself, "What in the world is Unhackable Favor, and how will it help me rewrite, reset, redo, and reclaim my story called life?"

I laughingly refer to myself as the farmer of the group. Before anything can grow, the soil must be cultivated. Hard, dry soil must be overturned. Weeds often need to be pulled. Fresh seeds are planted and watered before there is any sign of new life. Unhackable Favor begins with overturning the soil (emotions, attitudes, or beliefs) that has settled from the storms in life.

Let's begin by defining the word "favor." I believe it is best described as supernatural aid. Other words used to describe favor are approval, esteem, goodwill, kindness, benevolence, champion, support, blessing, godsend, and honor. You can see how closely favor and force are related. The goal of the

*Unhackable Force* movement is not only to empower ladies but to be an example of what can happen when fierce women come together with mutual respect, encouragement, power, truth, and vision (with a lot of fun thrown in the mix). Another word for favor that will appear from time to time is "boon."

In *Unhackable*, "boon" is described as a desire. Boons are big because they represent your deepest desire, your greatest ache, or your truest longing. As adults, most of us are disconnected from our heart's desire. Maybe at some point, we knew. But we've forgotten somewhere along the way. Desire is an interesting word. It literally means to give birth. Finding this desire is more about recovery than discovery.

I recognize the many places my life was hacked and my desires were lost. Painful events were entirely out of my control, while others resulted in the consequences of bad decisions. I never dreamed of being a career woman. I was all about a home full of children, pets, and constant activity. Yet, I have seen more success and favor in the corporate world. Many times, our focus to dig down to our deepest desires gets lost while trying to define the desire as something we do, a material thing we obtain, something we accomplish, or a lifestyle we live. That desire should rest with who we are, not with what we do or have.

Likewise, our life story is often written by the things we have endured. Your story is not what you are going through or what you have battled. This battle is not against who you have been. It is an all-out war against who you are becoming. You **are** your story. My life is not defined as the lady who lost four children. I am Deb. I am active and adventurous. I play tennis. I love encouraging others and seeing them embrace the next chapters of their lives. The circumstances in my life took me to the pits of sorrow and despair, which taught me the value of living every day to the fullest without being imprisoned to fear or the expectations of other people. **That** is my story.

Our story, as with life, is a journey, and the only constant is change. That is why circumstances or desired expectations can never completely be your story. Even those accomplishments you dreamed impossible will become history once they are met. I don't know a successful person who has "done" the same thing their entire adult life. Letting themselves continue to grow has opened doors of greater influence. How completely boring it would be to think there is one "duty" or purpose to life. As you grow, so do your opportunities.

What you thought was your greatest desire (such as being a wife and mother for me) may not be the way life rolls. Situations can be something that cannot be reclaimed. When I turned my focus to becoming the very best version of myself, doors began opening that were beyond anything I could have dreamed. That is the favor we are referring to in the section called Unhackable Favor. Your desire should be to become the very best *you*. The only way that can happen is by living a life of favor. Favor will surround you and begin clearing paths in front of you. There are two types of favor you will experience: the favor of God and the favor of man. The favor of man is natural, and the favor of God is reaching into supernatural aid.

Resetting, redoing, and reclaiming must always start with you, but it can never be accomplished by doing it alone. Favor enters our daily lives in many ways. You won't recognize the supernatural aid if you do not start with a heart of thankfulness for the blessings you can see. Gratitude is the greatest tool in your arsenal.

Living a life of favor and abundance doesn't just happen. It requires that you constantly search for truth and not settle for the lies that hack and derail. Your actions will always follow your thoughts. Don't let a moment become a mindset. Your thoughts must embrace truth, not lies, or the life of favor and abundance will escape you.

I felt like the decade of the 1990s would be better labeled as my decade from hell. I was raised with a very strong foundation.

When hell comes against you, regardless of your foundation, it will shake you to the core. One thought planted very early led to my imprisonment of the lie that God was against me instead of the truth that He was for me. I made the worst decision in my life in 1990 by having an abortion. It went against everything I believed from a spiritual aspect, and it totally went against my dreams of being a mother. I gave into fear and the feeling of abandonment. The following year, 1991, my father passed from cancer. It happened quickly. I began believing that if I hadn't had that abortion, my father would still be living. I viewed his death as divine payback.

I married in 1992 and became an instant mom to a precious ten-year-old boy. He had recently lost his mother to cancer as well. The husband, the child, and I brought a lot of grief into the new family dynamic. 1995 began as a year of hope. I was pregnant with another little boy. He made an early appearance and was stillborn. You can follow the details in my book *RISE...What To Do When Hell Won't Back Off.* To summarize briefly, holding that lifeless baby added to the lie I had already embraced: God was punishing me for the abortion. After a short time, I became pregnant again. Thirteen months later, I found myself back in the same maternity ward in the same hospital with the same doctors, telling me there were complications with the child I was carrying. That little boy was born alive but was only in our arms for an hour before he joined his brothers in Heaven.

Up until then, I had taken the losses with a dose of self-pity. This time, however, I was angry. I was angry at the doctors. Could they have missed something? I was angry at my choice to raise someone else's son when my own boys were immediately being yanked from my body. Most of all, I was angry at God. Who is this deity that calls himself *Love*?

The pain and tragedies continued. 1999 was life-changing. I had worked through the resentment of not having my own children and continued to love my stepson as my own. He took a small job to make extra money for a trip he had planned. His employer put him on a steel beam doing sheet roofing (something he had no experience doing) without providing any form of protection—no cables, belt, or hardhat! Two weeks before his twentieth birthday, my child fell twenty feet to his death on a slab of concrete.

*Come on, God! When is enough enough? Are you going to take everyone in my life just to get me back for a mistake I made?* Was I using God as a scapegoat because I wasn't ready to own the mistake I made against my dreams of being a mother?

As we continue to Day 8, we are going to go through the steps of releasing pain. Everyone's pain is different. It can take the form of disappointment, heartache, or tragedy. All pain can cause you to recoil from your passions and your life of favor.

I will add a scripture at the end of each day because I discovered a new foundation of God's love that rescued me. If that is not your foundation or belief, take the time to find an affirmation or quote for each day.

## BECOME A FORCE—DAY 2

1. Take an inventory and make a list of all the things in your life that you would like to do over. Don't edit your list. The items can be large or small. No over-thinking is allowed. Some things on your list may be choices you made. Some may be events out of your control. The list will not be shared with anyone, so complete transparency is required.

2. Now, take each item on your list and honestly answer this question. *Is this something I define myself by, or do I recognize this as something that happened in my life?* One way to know is by thinking about how many times you use that event or circumstance as a land-mark. For example, if you say things like, "Before

this or that happened" or "After such-and-such happened," most likely you are letting it define you.

It is important to keep in mind always as you go through these exercises, there is absolutely no condemnation for where you are. It is perfectly okay to feel exactly how you are feeling. There is no judgment in this space!

*Whenever our hearts make us feel guilty and remind us of our failures, we know God is much greater and more merciful than our conscience.*

—1 John 3:20 (TPT)

# DAY 3
## THOUGHTS ARE THE CULPRIT

*Rather than being your thoughts and emotions,*
*be the awareness behind them.*

—Eckhart Tolle

"Psychologists agree that we fear what we *can't* see even more than what we can see. Consider the scary times of 2020—fearing a virus we couldn't see. Or think back to the terrorist attacks of September 11, 2001, initiated by an invisible enemy.

For many people, their imaginations took over in both situations because they confronted a nameless or faceless threat. When we can't label the culprit, we can't *control* the culprit. Our vulnerability produces an unsettling feeling and gives our minds permission to fill in the blanks. This mental anguish produces psychological pain, often much more damaging than any physical pain. This prison of the mind holds us hostage, and we believe escape is no longer possible.

Thankfully, the opposite is true too. When we unmask our adversary, we immediately regain a sense of control. We know who or what threatens us and how we can defeat it. By discovering its weakness, we gain an edge that helps us outwit our opponent and ultimately defeat it."[3]

Unmasking the adversary isn't as easy as it may sound. The amount of information in this world doubles every twelve hours.[4] Note that it is information that doubles, not necessarily *truth*. Filtering the information could become an insurmountable task. We should ask ourselves the following questions:

- Where is the information coming from that I am absorbing?

- Is this information necessary?

- Will this information alter my convictions or beliefs?

- Does this information deserve space in my head?

- Is this information moving me toward progress?

- Do we really consider critically what we are thinking?

When coupled with the fact that our society is more sedentary than any previous generation, we are sitting ducks to become information sponges. Depression, anxiety, bitterness, anger, fear, rejection, hopelessness, loneliness, rebellion, temptation, and many other conditions begin in the mind. These things can control our lives unless we take the reins of our thoughts. Unmasking truth and hope during a season of pain is like walking through a minefield. Triggers come from every direction. "It's a known fact that thoughts create emotions, and emotions create actions which in turn create results. Often, when we hear the word 'results,' we think of a positive outcome. But are all 'results' good?"[5]

Our thoughts and emotions have many origins. Time has proven that one specific thought in the mind of a hurting person is a strong predictor of becoming stuck. That thought is one simple word. That one simple word can enter your mind like a feather floating in the wind and quickly turn into a hurricane-sized gale of torment. Have you figured it out? That word is *why*.

Why? Why? Why? There are so many questions that encircle loss. The pain, heartaches, disappointments, and death we face on this earth leave us desperately seeking. Uncertainty leads to the pursuit of truth. We spend time in therapy sessions, spiritual counseling, and books upon books looking for answers. We may find some level of acceptance for the pain, but we will never fully understand it.

Without those answers, it would be natural to feel the need to blame someone. We initially tend to blame those closest to us, the ones who love us most. The emotions must spill out somewhere, and our safe place to dump them is commonly where we will not face rejection. (Anger will come at a later stage, and it can explode anywhere on anyone.)

So, how do you begin to take control over this culprit in your head? I will forewarn you. If you are looking for a quick fix, this book is *not* it! It can be simple, but it is not easy. If you are into being the best you can be, improving your relationships, businesses, and lifestyle, then the path outlined in this book will be for you. It takes lots of patience and effort to gain a life of favor.

The truth inside your thoughts will set you free. Most of our damaging thoughts are programmed lies. Is there anything you have believed all your life, and you don't know why? An example could be a food you don't eat, but you can't remember ever eating it. You have always simply "known" you don't like it.

Is there an opinion you have about yourself that came from someone else's words or actions toward you? Remember, when someone puts you down or treats you inappropriately, the problem lies somewhere deep inside of them, not with you.

If you root out the damaging lies with truth, your life of favor will begin to blossom. Your life can be reclaimed and your story rewritten.

# BECOME A FORCE—DAY 3

1. Make a list of things in life you have a strong opinion about—certain foods, situations, activities, etc. Think of something you would immediately say no to. Now, take each item, and give your documented reason for it. How many things have you experienced? How do you let programmed thoughts keep you from knowing the truth behind it or perhaps give into fear? Now, try doing some of these things to discover if it is as bad as your thoughts had convinced you.

2. Make a list of your opinions and thoughts about yourself. It is common for all the negative thoughts to dump out first. Take each one of those thoughts and counteract it with an objective truth about yourself. Did that thought come from someone else? If it is a physical attribute, is there something you can do to change it?

*Hope deferred makes my heart sick, but when my desire is fulfilled, it is a tree of life.*

—Proverbs 13:12 (AMP)

# DAY 4
## YOU ARE A.B.L.E.

*I want you to have it all . . . all you can imagine.*

—Jason Mraz

What is your reason for moving past pain to rewrite your story? Ask yourself these questions:

1. Why do I want life to change?

2. What is my idea of wholeness?

3. What will life look like after healing and transformation occur?

To be complete and move forward, you must know the answer to those questions. Without the perceived end, I guarantee you will get stuck somewhere along the way. Do not settle for partial transformation.

Healing from pain can be deceptive. As a society, we are so accustomed to finding a comfort zone and camping there. The pattern becomes evident with grief and support groups.

Not all groups reflect that, but for the most part, the ones I have been acquainted with have operated in this fashion. It can end up supporting grief instead of moving past it.

Rewriting your story begins in a state of brokenness. When a person initiates a search to release pain, they have most likely reached a deep point where they realize change must occur. Most have already tried other sources to numb the pain, which can range from religion to rebellion.

The bottom of the pit in life can look different based on experiences. For some, it may be an extreme disappointment from an unfulfilled expectation. For others, it is a heartache from a shift in life after investing heart, soul, and time. Then there are tragedies outside our control that leave us in shock and wondering if life is even worth continuing. Regardless, when you begin your journey of wholeness, the only direction from your consciousness is up.

Many people see healing or recovery as a journey; I see it more as a climb. Having grown up in the Smoky Mountains, I have logged many hours on those trails. There is nothing more beautiful and strenuous at the same time.

While speaking with a group in Dallas, I shared the following story to illustrate my point. I was hiking to Laurel Falls as a child. The trail is only a mile and an easy climb. The path has been paved to make it easier for children or possibly even someone in a wheelchair to enjoy the sense of accomplishment as they ascend the trail. I thought I had successfully reached a prominent summit and was playing in the waterfall. Little did I know, on the other side of the mountain, The Chimneys would be a new climb that challenged more of me. The view at the top would be breathtaking and beyond anything I had experienced.

So it is with rewriting your story and becoming a force. When you are at the lowest point, any achievement is fulfilling and should be fully absorbed. Breathe it. Smell it. Embrace it—but don't set up camp. If I had stayed at Laurel Falls, I would have missed the summit of the Chimneys. Sure, it would have been satisfying, but I was only halfway up the mountain. I was still surrounded by tall trees where I could barely see the sky, but the water was refreshing. I had made progress on the climb, and I could have settled for a partial view from a partial summit. Healing offers similar places to stop along the way. Unless we have a destination in mind, we can miss the most beautiful scenes and the wholeness that awaits. I will not lie to you. It is not easy. I can also promise you that at some point, you will recognize a seamless transition from your pain into a new life waiting to be explored.

As you take your beginning steps to rewrite your story, you will feel some stretching. The most important part of transformation (or any colossal task) is knowing when to rest and refresh. It is appropriate to rest on the rock or broken tree trunk, but do not mistake it for your destination. Catch your breath and keep going.

You may reach a plateau on your climb. That can become the most jeopardizing location. It seems you can finally relax. This place is precisely where someone can become stuck on the healing journey. You have exhausted all your energy and done all you know to do. You feel so much further along than the place you began. But is this all there is? Is this your greatest desire? Is there room for a big dose of favor?

I had reached a point where I thought I was healed. I had fully accepted the death of my children and the loss of my home and marriage. I had even written my first book to encourage other people to survive tragedies and enjoy their life still, but that healing was only a partial transformation.

I was living in Kentucky at the time and felt a nudge to move back to Ohio—the place of pain, where I lost everything and where hope began and was destroyed. I tried to push the thought away, but it kept getting stronger. I had a "come to Jesus moment" about leaving a place I loved and moving back to the place that, for me, represented nothing but defeat, but I knew I must go.

The supernatural aid of favor began almost immediately. I was randomly connected with the lady in charge of the labor and delivery ward in the hospital where my babies were born. She invited me to meet her at the hospital. Reluctantly, I went. She shared with me that the hospital now had a beautiful garden of remembrance. Inside the garden, pavers were placed with the names of babies born in the hospital but who went to heaven instead of going home with their parents. Keep in mind my visit was twenty-two years after my sons were born. She asked if I would like to have a memorial service and have markers placed bearing my sons' names.

It was a beautiful ceremony. My mom and five of my closest girlfriends who experienced the babies' births with me attended. (The details are in my book RISE..What To Do When Hell Won't Back OFF.) We never had a funeral for the babies, so this ceremony was a welcome gesture. God knew I needed some closure, and my sons now have a place marked for their remembrance. I had no idea scar tissue surrounded that wound. I had no idea the depth of peace I would experience after the memorial for my sons.

As I mentioned earlier, the biggest mistake of my life was having an abortion. After moving to Ohio, I connected with a faith-based pregnancy crisis center and became friends with the ladies who ran it. They, too, had a garden of remembrance. I was offered the opportunity to place a plaque in the garden with my aborted son's name on it and have a small memorial service. The ceremony was intimate and precious, attended only by me, my mom, and a counselor at the center. Another layer of scar tissue was removed from around my heart.

I share these experiences only to say that a life of favor begins inside your pain. Do not be afraid to revisit pain. Do not be afraid to let it hurt. Do not be afraid to admit that all you know to do is not all that can be done.

You are able to rewrite your story. You are able to receive the supernatural aid you need. You are able to live a life of favor. You are able to become a force. During the next four days, we are going to explore four steps to move you forward. (*To receive a free guide of these steps to a life of favor and other free bonuses, go to UnhackableForce.com.*)

A = Awareness
B = Brokenness
L = Leverage
E = Expectation

## BECOME A FORCE—DAY 4

1. Identify your pain—from your list on Day 2, choose one thing to address during the next four days. It will most likely be the one thing or event you were reluctant to write—the one that caused so much pain you didn't even want to raise it. It could also be the one causing an embarrassing moment that left you with an identity from a moment that turned into a mindset (you will share this with no one).

2. Focus on the details of your choice. Write down how it immediately changed your life or way of thinking. Then write the ways it continues to do so.

3. Now, write in detail how a complete transformation in that area would look. Focus on the word *complete*. Be bold; be courageous; be wild, and be brave. Don't hold back.

*I will give you a new heart and put a new spirit within you, and I will remove the heart of stone from your flesh and give you a heart of flesh.*

—Ezekiel 36:26 (AMP).

# DAY 5

## AWARENESS

*Denial is the ultimate comfort zone.*

—Dave Goggins

I've laid a lot of groundwork in Days 2-4. Now it's your turn to do some digging and begin reclaiming and rewriting your story.

The next four days will require you to be calculated. Because we have a dream for something doesn't mean we will get there. It's like planning a trip; we can make all the travel plans in the world, but unless we intentionally get in a car, plane, or ship and move toward it, we will never see the destination. So, hang with us through these thirty days of becoming an *Unhackable Force*. You are not alone.

There is a huge difference between self-improvement and transformation. Self-improvement often works behind a mask. Transformation removes the mask.

Are you trying to improve while staying behind your mask? I did that for years. It is limiting and gains few lasting results. Transformation requires vulnerability and the willingness to be broken.

The first step is to become aware of exactly where you are emotionally, physically, mentally, spiritually, financially—everywhere.

> When a person is not totally aware of the things that trigger certain actions, reactions, thoughts, and feelings, life will ultimately control them instead of them controlling their life. Being aware of what triggers certain thoughts and feelings is the start of controlling and changing them whenever necessary.[6]

Again, I want you to focus only on the item you chose from Day 2 as we go through the next four days.

The first awareness most people deal with is **fear.** Fear goes right back to our discussion during Day 2. The unknown and unseen can often be the biggest threats we face. The greatest playground fear has is our mind and our thoughts. I can get myself all worked up with imaginings. I will have a threatening idea that will lead to a greater one, which will create a scenario that will fill in all the imaginary details of the scenario, which then plants the seeds of defeat. I have, at that point, gotten depressed or given up on my original idea. Nothing I was thinking was real, but fear got stronger with each thought, and I was reacting as if I was living it out.

Did you know your nervous system does not know the difference between reality and imagination? Your body *will* respond to your thoughts. So, whether you think of something from your past or borrow negativity from your future, your body will react the same way. You could see a difference in anxiety, blood pressure, or breathing. You could put unfair pressure on your nervous system. **Keep it real.** When those fearful thoughts come, retract them and replace them with the reality of the moment. The best way to do that is with gratitude.

Throughout history, we have been warned that the only thing to fear is fear itself.

1580: *"The thing I fear most is fear."* Michel de Montaigne, *French Essayist/Writer*

1623: *"Nothing is terrible except fear itself."* Francis Bacon, *English Author and Statesman*

1831: *"The only thing I am afraid of is fear."* The Duke of *Wellington*

1851: *"Nothing is so much to be feared as fear."* Henry *David Thoreau*

1933: *"The only thing we have to fear is fear itself."* Franklin *D Roosevelt*

You were not born with fear. Let's become childlike and approach life with abandonment instead of fear and timidity. Do not be afraid of change as you rewrite your story and reclaim your life. Once truth hits our brain, we do not automatically have the strength and courage to make changes. Nothing changes when we sit and hope. The perfect doors will open if we are willing to take the first steps. Daphne is going to go deeper with you about giving yourself permission. Part of that is giving yourself the permission to change. Why is change so frightening? Fear of change is only fear of loss.

Let's look at the fear of loss from two perspectives.

- *Losing something or someone you currently have possession of:* Wow! I feel like I have written that story way too many times. I have already shared my losses both here and in *RISE*, so I will move on to what I learned in the process. First and foremost, we do not possess

32

anything or anyone. One of the greatest mistakes is to hold on too tightly. Be careful who or what you give your heart to because whatever happens to what you are attached to will also happen to your heart.

- **What you might lose if you stay stuck and never move toward your dream or never rewrite your story to become an Unhackable Force living a life of favor:** "Rather than focusing on what I *might gain* if I implemented my idea, I flipped my focus. I invested time in thinking about what I *might lose* if I permanently got hacked."[7] There is so much joy and so many blessings you will lose in life if your choice is not to take the first step. You can never win a battle you refuse to fight.

The second awareness that needs to be addressed is **the ability to keep it real.** To go higher, you must go deeper. As you ponder over the area of your life you want to reclaim, you must be honest with yourself.

Confession is freeing. Sometimes you must let go of the picture of what you thought life would be and find joy in the life you are living. **The disappointments, heartaches, and traumas of yesterday will speak if nothing interrupts.**

I will share a personal awareness with you to lighten this conversation a bit. I spent five years caring for my mother before she passed. During that time, I let myself go. It was a hard season to live through, and I am an emotional eater. The weight piled on. But the problem was that the only mirrors in my house were reflecting from the waist up. I wasn't aware of just how large my butt and thighs had gotten. The first time Daphne, Lisa, Niccie, and I spent a few days strategizing about this book, we did a photo shoot. I was mortified when I saw the pictures. In my perception, those three girls looked like Barbie® dolls, and I looked like Shamu. They didn't see it that way (probably because they were aware of what the full-length view of me looked like). What an "awareness" slap in the face for me! The first thing I did was buy a full-length mirror. I could not go through the pain and process of reclaiming my body unless I was aware of how it looked.

Honesty leads to vulnerability. Transformation takes place in the brokenness. We are going to take a deep dive into brokenness on Day 6. The caterpillar could continue learning different ways to crawl but ask the butterfly if the brokenness was worth the freedom to fly. (*To receive a free guide of these steps to a life of favor and other free bonuses, go to UnhackableForce.com.*)

## BECOME A FORCE—DAY 5

1. Identify your fears! This is another place where you will not edit. If it goes through your mind, write it down. This is a safe place, and you do not have to share it with anyone.

   Here are a few places to start. Is there anything you are afraid of losing? Is there something you are afraid of becoming? Is there someone you are afraid of being vulnerable with? What is the worst-case scenario going through your mind right now?

2. Take each fear you identified, and write a paragraph exposing your true, raw, and honest emotions about it. You can write to the universe. You can write to someone if there is a particular person entangled in your fear. Take this opportunity to be open with your emotions.

   *Open up before God. Hold nothing back.*
   *He'll do whatever needs to be done!*

   —Psalm 37 (MSG)

# Day 6
## BROKENNESS

*The truth is that it hurts because it's real.*
*It hurts because it mattered.*

*And that's an important thing to acknowledge to yourself.*

—John Greene

"**B**reathe it in until your heart breaks, then exhale!"[8] This will undoubtedly be the hardest day, but I promise you, it will be the most rewarding if you press on. With each retreat and workshop I lead, the topic of brokenness has proven to be the pivotal point of transformation.

Resist the temptation to act like it doesn't hurt. You must let it hurt to get to the other side of the pain. That is where many people get stuck. Our emotions and bodies were designed to go through a mourning process, but our society often tells us to stop the process. Letting it hurt will bring the freedom to reclaim and rewrite the story of your life and move toward a life of favor.

Mentally, our bodies are programmed to go through a specific sequence of emotional states following emotional trauma or stress. Grieving and mourning are completely natural and necessary states that your brain processes through in order to move past events and work through the realities of life. This explains why people that are temporarily relieved of their depression by antidepressant medication eventually end up chronically depressed. Their brain never went through the appropriate process necessary to establish peace with the situation.

The first steps of the process are the worst. I hate to inform you that when you are going through what can seem an endless season of disappointments, heartache, and grief, you will face the deepest parts alone. There will be windows where loving friends will encourage you and even pray with you, but dark nights and early mornings will find you alone with your thoughts. For the moment, this is the best place to be. Do not attach your healing or transformation to a person. You must face the temporary darkness in solitude. This is where your next chapter begins, and only you can write it.

Butterflies are beautiful and graceful. Healed people who have taken the time to feel the brokenness are beautiful as they manifest peace and favor. In both cases, no one sees what it actually took for these metamorphoses to occur.

*Metamorphosis* is defined as "the process of transformation from an immature form to an adult form in two or more distinct stages."[9] Did you catch that? Two or more stages! Another definition is "a change of the form or nature of a thing or person into a completely different one by natural and/or supernatural means."[10]

Let's look at the caterpillar and the butterfly. Have you ever thought about what takes place while the caterpillar is inside the dark cocoon and in the process of transformation?

The life of a butterfly has four stages—egg, larva, pupa, and adult. It is easy to relate these stages to our own transformation.

- **Egg**: Our birth occurs with its own unique beauty. We are all designed with individual DNA. We experience different cultures, families, and life experiences.

- **Larva:** This is referred to as the caterpillar stage. I find this stage fascinating because every scientific article I read about larva states that the main purpose of the caterpillar is to eat. It goes through about five cycles of eating and shedding its skin. As it eats, it becomes too large for its skin, so it sheds and grows into a new one. Yet, it remains a caterpillar.

So, it is with our story. As we walk through the pages of our life, it seems circumstances cause us to "eat" or absorb the storms of life. We learn; we cope; we grow. Yet, we remain stuck. We seem to be inching along. We measure little amounts of progress and growth. Each "new skin" provides a new life lesson but not a lot of transformation. We need a new chapter.

"A caterpillar spends most of its time eating. Hormonal changes occur, and the caterpillar loses interest in feeding. When it's time to become an adult, it finds a sheltered safe spot where it transforms itself."[11]

"In your healing journey you will outgrow friends. This is normal and ok."[12]

- **Pupa:** This is it! Transformation at last. A new chapter begins.

The caterpillar finds a "sheltered safe spot." The transformation does not take place in public view. **Brokenness** takes place within **boundaries.** We, too, must place boundaries around ourselves in order to achieve a complete transformation. These boundaries may include pulling away from negative people, coming off social media, or going somewhere for that much-needed getaway. Only you can decide what you need to step away from to find your safe space.

During this stage, it will appear the caterpillar is resting in the tightly woven cocoon, but the inside is where all the action is. It is completely torn apart, and a new body is formed.

"The change itself inside the chrysalis is slow and gradual. The caterpillar's body digests itself from the inside out. The caterpillar is attacked by the same juices used in its earlier life to digest food. Many organs hidden in the caterpillar take on a new form within the chrysalis."[13]

Not to be gross, but literally, the juices completely melt and digest the body of the caterpillar. Do not be surprised if you feel slightly nauseated! There is a complete DNA exchange happening. It will hurt to let go of mistaken and misguided thoughts that have formed your identity. Remember, anything you feel you are losing during this process will be replaced with something better. Dealing with the memory of a loved one can be a little different during this stage. You may have to cry it out. Let the void scream with each memory. You will get to the place where those memories will bring comfort and smiles.

There is no way to make this stage of transformation as uniform for us as it is for the butterfly. Each person's soul is formed by the experiences they have. It is much like peeling back layers. Your healing and transformation will be as unique as the circumstances you have experienced. Your boundaries and cocoon will provide your safe place to experience the transformation.

- **Adult:** Finally, when the caterpillar has done all its forming and changing inside the cocoon, it will emerge slowly. There is no big "ta-da!" moment. It has been closed within a tight dark space. It has grown wings but never experienced the lift of flight. It is interesting to point out that the butterfly never

goes back to the ground to crawl around with cater-
pillars. It accepts and inhabits the new body.

We, too, must emerge slowly after our brokenness. We must
learn to walk in our newness. The new body of the butterfly
was designed for a completely new life with different experiences. It allows the butterfly to function as it was designed
from the beginning.

It's staying with the breaking that produces the blessing!
(*To receive a free guide of these steps to a life of favor and other
free bonuses, go to UnhackableForce.com.*)

## BECOME A FORCE—DAY 6

1. Set Your Boundaries: Identify obstacles that may
   be blocking your opportunity to begin the new
   chapter in your transformation and find your safe
   space. Know things or people you will need to avoid.
   Obstacles come in many shapes and sizes. Some
   could be well-meaning people, yet they could slow
   us down to the point we would never go through
   our metamorphosis. Other obstacles could be activities that steal our time and prevent us from moving
   through our pain to our freedom.

2. Rest: That seems like an odd request, doesn't it?
   During the deepest dark, the quietest solitude, and
   the abrasive brokenness, I tell you to rest? Yes! That
   is the only way you will see a transformation. If you
   try to do it yourself, trust me, you will screw the
   process up. (Ask me how I know.) Even though you
   are alone during the process, it is the perfect time
   to lean into the guidance and direction of the Holy
   Spirit. Remember, during the pupa stage, it appears
   from the outside as if nothing is happening. Yet, on

the inside, the caterpillar is allowing itself to be torn apart. It's such a paradox.

*If your heart is broken, you'll find God right there; if you are kicked in the gut, he'll help you catch your breath.*

—Psalm 34 (MSG).

# DAY 7
## LEVERAGE

*Great things are done by a series of
small things brought together.*

—Vincent Van Gogh

I trust you survived Day 6. Welcome to Day 7. Life is a journey, so you will see the results from Day 6 for days, weeks, months, and years to come.

Today we are going to focus on leveraging what you learned from your brokenness. One of the taglines I have used for years has been Unmasking Hope/Embracing Life. Working through the brokenness to find wholeness is only the beginning. We unmask the hope inside to give us the strength and courage to embrace life all around us. As we discussed earlier, there must be a reason you desire to be whole in the specific area you chose to work. What will life look like when that wholeness is achieved?

Once your mind and emotions are clear, and you have discovered the peace you weren't sure even existed, it is time to take the next steps. These steps will begin small because you are a new creature. You now have wings, and your horizon is limitless.

Do not be afraid of small beginnings. It will take time for the finished picture to be revealed. One small step can open the door for a huge leap toward the dream that has been inside you for years. But we must take that first step.

I'll share a personal story of small steps working through financial ruin. My solid belief is that you should do something for yourself each time you get paid. Not everything you earn should go to bills. Trust me, I was living from paycheck to paycheck, and there was always something waiting for every penny. A mentor of mine taught me years ago to always celebrate yourself. It doesn't have to cost a lot of money, but it must be intentional. It could be a movie matinee, a picnic in the park, or anything that brings you joy. With each paycheck, I went to a local store and spent $10 on myself. I bought a bouquet of fresh flowers for $5. I bought a private label bottle of wine for $3 (if you drink wine, you will know where I was shopping when I say the wine was referred to as Two Buck Chuck) and a bar of dark chocolate for $2. So, for $10, I treated myself to flowers, wine, and chocolate. *I was worth it.*

It was a small step in moving away from financial ruin. I could have paid every penny toward a bill, but I deserved to feel rewarded for my work to keep making progress. What are you doing to celebrate yourself?

Let's look again at *Unhackable.*

Are you too big to take on small assignments? What if those small assignments are in alignment with your ultimate idea? In my experience, Big Boons are often achieved through a series of small steps. David's past successes convinced King Saul to promote him to a bigger future. Facing the giant and then killing the giant was a result of saying yes to smaller assignments. These small assignments—killing the lion and bear—went largely unnoticed. (His sheep may have been the only ones who saw it.) Yet because David prepared for the moment, the moment was prepared for him. Eventually, the world realized what the world already knew—that he was ready for a bigger stage.[14]

Another example of leverage after pain is in the familiar Prayer of Jabez found in 1 Chronicles 4. His mother named him Jabez because his birth was so painful. He was the one who prayed to the God of Israel, "'Oh, that You would bless me indeed, and enlarge my territory, that Your hand would be with me, and that You would keep me from evil, that I may not cause pain!' So God granted him what he requested." (NKJV)

A quick examination of this section of Scripture shows that pain does not have to be directly experienced for it to affect you. There are many circumstances in life where we don't take the direct hit, but we certainly live with the consequences. The fact that his mother named him after the birth experience shows she always wanted him to be aware of the pain he caused. My interpretation is certainly not based on a deep theological study, but I can't help but wonder a few things. Did he cry out to God to bless him and expand his territory to move away from his constant reminder that he was a pain? Did he have a sincere heart to live a life in the favor of God by asking God to be with him in all that he did? Had his life been so shadowed with talk of pain and trouble that he just wanted a life free from the reminder of the pain he was labeled with?

I leave it up to you to answer these questions. There is no denying the boldness in Jabez as he brought his honesty and desires to God—and God granted his request. It doesn't appear there was a lot of debate about it. The text simply says his requests were granted. What I see in this is that Jabez was ready for his favor. He was prepared for his influence to be larger. Apparently, he had graciously walked under the shadow of pain and been faithful in the small things. Then, one day he may have realized, like the caterpillar, he was born to fly.

## BECOME A FORCE—DAY 7

1. Take inventory of the small things. Is there anything you have said no to because you are waiting for the bigger opportunity or stage? Are there any pressing ideas you have not pursued that could possibly open bigger doors? Do you have dreams so big you honestly don't know where the first step is?

2. Make your plan. Take that big dream and define the first step. It may be a business startup or expansion, and you need to put a strategy in place. It may be that vacation you always dreamed of, and you need to start reading travel brochures. It may be you are finally ready to take a health and wellness plan seriously, and you need to buy a full-length mirror. (lol) Do not be afraid to be bold in your plan and your prayers.

*In kindness he takes us firmly by the hand*
*and leads us into a radical life change.*

—Romans 2 (MSG)

# DAY 8

## EXPECTATIONS

*You only live once, but if you do it right, once is enough.*

—Unknown

I am super excited to share Day 8 because it is my favorite day—not because you made it through Days 2–7, but because this is where you can begin to see the favor you've never imagined. You will begin your rewritten life when you start thinking about expectations. As I mentioned in Day 2, I found a solid spiritual foundation after mine was crushed to the core. I have experienced the love of God, and there is no debate about it. I am giving you a peek inside of that love today.

Just as you don't settle for partial transformation, you don't settle for partial blessings. This can be my biggest frustration as I help people reclaim their lives and rewrite their stories—their expectations remain extremely small.

John 10:10 brings such clarity throughout several translations. "I came so that they can have real and eternal life, more and better life than they ever dreamed of." (MSG) "My purpose is to give them a rich and satisfying life." (NLT) "But

I have come to give you everything in abundance, more than you expect—life in its fullness until you overflow!" (TPT) "I came that they may have and enjoy life, and have it in abundance." (AMP)

I used to think abundance meant you had everything you needed and enough left over to help someone else. I now know that abundance means the freedom you have inside your heart when you literally embrace the adventurous ride God has planned for you.

Abundance is not a net worth. Abundance doesn't come as a reward or consolation prize for a trial or battle we have endured. It is a mindset and lifestyle we learn to expect.

Once people move past their pain, they begin to walk the road to abundance and a life of favor. However, they often stop somewhere along the way. Comfort is confused with achievement. In Ephesians, the Bible says that He is able to do over and above all we could ask or think. I love the way the message says: "God can do anything, you know—far more than you could ever imagine or guess or request in your wildest dreams! He does it not by pushing us around but by working within us, his Spirit deeply and gently within us." Ephesians 3:20 (MSG)

I don't know about you, but I can dream big and ask for a lot! What would happen in our lives if we continued to imagine, guess, or request from God once we had reached our comfort levels?

When we see one intervention of supernatural aid that is above and beyond all we could ask or think, it is easy to relax instead of remaining expectant for more. Does God ever run out of favor? I don't think so.

When we begin to measure or track progress toward our dream, we must take time out of the equation. When we have big ideas, we must have deep roots to support them, and it takes time for those roots to grow. As with metamorphosis, the butterfly does not appear overnight.

I make it a point to celebrate progress, regardless of the size. The truth is, most of the time, the progress of an idea is slow—so slow most people miss it or mock it. It's understandable why we get discouraged. After all, we exert mountains of effort for very little impact—at least on the surface. But don't be fooled. Much is going on beneath the surface. During this testing time, our ideas dig deep roots. This depth is essential because, without deep roots, our ideas can't support the weight of their impact once you break through the surface. *Deep roots mean rich fruits.*[15]

As you are rewriting, resetting, redoing, and reclaiming your story, keep in mind that there is always more. There is always a new chapter waiting to be written, and each chapter will become more abundant than the last. One of my favorite songs is from a few years ago by Danny Gokey titled "More Than You Think I Am." Even though it is referring to God. No matter how well you may feel you know God or how much you think you know about God......He is more than that. It is the same with you. (We were made in his image after all...). No matter what you have accomplished, no matter what your life has looked like up until now, good or bad.....**You Are More!**

There is a beautiful, sweet spot when you are in alignment with the life of favor. I will not even entertain the idea that it is not possible. Facts can be debated, but an experience cannot. I am watching God do supernatural and unexpected things to restore my life. I have reclaimed my value from feeling worthless and replaceable. I have reclaimed my hope of a bright future instead of looking behind at the loss. I have even seen God part the waters for me financially and restore every penny I lost plus more. I no longer see lack in my life. I no longer see despair and disappointment. I see promise and excitement. I'm just waiting to see what's going to happen next.

One of my favorite verses is ironically found in the book of Job. I have tried and tested God on this verse, and He has come through every time. "After all, he's famous for great and unexpected acts: There is no end to His surprises." Job 5:9 (MSG) Have you ever asked God for a surprise? Have you ever expected Him to give you something unplanned or unexpected? Do it! Do it NOW!

You see, that is how I now live my life. I went from believing God was a thief to laughing with Him daily. My peace and favor are found in the freedom of an abundant relationship with Him. That is why my greatest joy is to play a small part in taking someone drowning in pain and deception to a place of joy and the abundant living they were designed for. (*To make a deeper connection with me or allow me to walk you through the process, find me at UnhackableForce.com.*)

I am going to wrap this part up with a couple of personal examples that show unexpected favor. I had a speaking engagement in Ft. Myers, Florida, followed by another a few days later in Jacksonville, Florida. I had decided to drive from one city to the next and stopped for some relaxation time in Orlando at Walt Disney World˚. At that time, the Animal Kingdom had just opened.

The Animal Kingdom was the only park I hadn't visited, so I decided to buy a ticket for the afternoon. The lady selling the ticket was very concerned that I did not have the full day and could not return the next day to enjoy the park. She kept reminding me what time the park closed and how limited my time was. I assured her I understood and would do what I could to enjoy my time there. I asked her what exhibits or rides she would not miss if her time were limited. Her voice was kind as she said, "Hold on a minute, I'll be right back."

I thought she would get a map for me to scout out and plan my few hours. Instead, she came back with a VIP pass and said, "I just want to give this to you to enjoy your day." I was able to go right in front of the line at every ride and exhibit. I think I did the entire Animal Kingdom twice.

I realize her gesture was not a life-changing event, but I want to impress upon you that favor, and surprises come in all sizes. I saw that VIP pass as a wink from God.

On a larger scale, I did have a life-changing event. My mother was a beneficiary of a trust fund that did not carry to the next generation. The owner of the fund passed ten months before my mother. Because of the timing, Mom was due the funds, and I received them into my mother's estate after she passed. The amount completely changed my lifestyle. I would give back every penny to have these two precious ladies back in my life. But since that is not an option, I am grateful for the favor God showed to me through their lives.

Confucius said, "Man who chases two rabbits, catches none." You can't entertain thoughts of doubt and expectation at the same time. Choose Expectations! Choose Favor!

## BECOME A FORCE—DAY 8

What is your greatest dream, desire, or boon? Are you expecting it? Have you written it down? Have you put a time frame on it? Have you taken steps toward it? Have you shared it with trusted people?

Are you filling the gap to reset, redo, and reclaim a life of favor?

You get two Scriptures today.

*After all, he's famous for great and unexpected acts:*
*There is no end to His Surprises.*

—Job 5:9 (MSG)

*She laughs without fear of the future.*

—Proverbs 31:25 (NLT)

# PART 2

## UNHACKABLE
## OPPORTUNITY

# DAY 9
## RESOLVE

*If something's not working, try something different.*

—Daphne V Smith

It's not about working harder. Let's be clear; harder does not always equal better or faster results. It does mean expending more energy and paying a higher cost.

So the questions that come to mind are, how committed are you, and what price are you willing to pay?

Are you so resolved, dedicated, and bought into your dream that you're willing to risk push back?

One of my favorite sayings is *dogs bark at what they don't understand.* When you make a true commitment to your goal, dream, boon, or acceptance of favor, be prepared. Some people are not going to be as thrilled as you are.

It doesn't mean they don't love you, approve of you, or want the best for you. It does mean they are concerned for themselves and how your choice is going to affect them. How will your choice change their lives and options? Imagine every other person in your world wearing or holding a sign asking, what about me?

Obviously, I'm not trying to win the approval of others but of God. If pleasing people were my goal, I would not be Christ's servant. I would not be a servant of Christ. (Galatians 1:10, NLT)

The DSV or Daphne Smith Version of this quote simply means you're not going to please everyone if you're focused on pleasing The One.

It's impossible to please everyone all the time. Even Jesus didn't make everyone happy. So, guess what? You're off the hook. Repeat after me: It's not my problem.

You can't control another person's thoughts or words; that is evident from social media trolls and online haters. You can, however, control how you respond or choose not to. When you are self-controlled, what others say really can bounce off like a Nerf dart. They can shoot all kinds of venomous and hurtful words your way, and with a strong resolve, you will barely even notice the assault.

Years ago, when I entered the world of recovery, one of the first principles I learned was *what someone else thinks of me is none of my business.*

It was a bit shocking and, honestly, a bit of a relief. The idea helped me realize some independence, and I no longer needed to concern myself with the perceptions of others. I didn't need to justify, explain, or defend my choices—and neither do you! When you break the chains keeping you stuck in people-pleasing, you begin to truly take authorship and ownership of your life.

Spending my time on gaining the approval of others (and newsflash, it's simply impossible with some) is giving them my power. It's allowing them to control me. And I don't know about you, but my inner two-year-old doesn't want to be controlled. Does yours?

Somewhere along this journey of life, we started caring more about what others thought of us than what our hearts guided us toward. It's the boiling frog syndrome.

When a frog is removed from its natural habitat and placed into a pot of water filled with the same temperature they just left, as long as the heat on the stove is turned up gradually enough, it won't even try to jump out. It will remain in that pot until it is boiled to death.

We can be a bit like frogs at times. The slow fade, the gradual acceptance of another's opinion or limiting beliefs can have a detrimental influence on our choices and beliefs.

Once you have decided or resolved yourself to achieve your dream, you're going to need to find ways to silence both the inner and outer critics who try to dissuade you.

Equipping yourself keeps the power and energy where it belongs—within. A sure-fire way to do so is through enthusiasm.

Enthusiasm doesn't mean you're always going to feel like a head cheerleader or hype girl. Enthused stems from the Greek, inspired or possessed by God. When we are enthused, we have a cellular level of commitment. It becomes ingrained.

Picture a piece of wood. Or even better, if time allows, find a piece. Look at the natural patterns that make up the grain. The swirls, lines, even knot holes are part of what makes each type and piece of wood unique. That is what helps define, identify, and distinguish the wood's beauty and purpose.

Every decision you make has a price. For each person you make happy, you'll disappoint someone else. So, how about making yourself the happiest? By doing so, you're giving others permission to do the same.

As you grow through the rest of your *Unhackable Force* experience, allow yourself to consider the energy you're applying to a goal, relationship, or dream. Letting go or altering your vision and expectation could be the healthiest option.

Remember, every yes is also a no.

## BECOME A FORCE—DAY 9

For today's assignment, answer these questions:

1. What do I consider my top three priorities?

2. How much time do I invest in nurturing them?

3. What am I holding onto that is not producing good, healthy fruit? These could be habits, relationships, or beliefs.

4. How much more time and energy am I willing to invest in them?

5. Where is there a disconnect between my priorities and my investment?

6. What am I willing to replace or let go? What will I resolve to change?

# Day 10

## CREATE

*You can't do epic stuff surrounded by basic people.*

—Daphne V. Smith

What woman hasn't wistfully hoped for more days or hours to get everything done?

Truth be told, more is not the answer. Sometimes less *is* more. Think about the classic example of an out-of-town friend or in-law calling (or in our modern world sending a text or snap) to announce their arrival in a few short minutes. How fast can you pull it together?

I've been amazed at how fast I can clean, straighten, and organize before someone important or special arrives on short notice. This can include our desk and office if a corporate setting applies. When the department head or vice president decides to drop in unannounced, how fast do we devise creative ways to present ourselves?

The answer lies within clearing to create. Once you've addressed the "stuff" that's keeping you stuck, your entire being is open and free.

Today, I will share with you a portion of what I walk my personal clients through when they experience being stuck. It's a four-step process to clean out what's keeping you blocked or in an endless holding pattern.

We all toddle before we walk. The challenge can come when we're afraid to get back up again after the most recent tumble. What keeps a toddler committed to getting up and trying again? They don't know any better! They assume they have what it takes, and they simply need to figure out the process. They're not familiar with the concept of failing, so they keep going.

To understand, claim, and embrace your favor, you'll need to clear out what's blocking it. I refer to that stuff as C.R.A.P.

- **C**haos: The things keeping you off-center, sucking your energy, and distracting you.

  When we live in chaos (and since we keep things real here, it's most likely our own doing), we don't set ourselves up to receive what's best and intended for us. Instead, we settle for dealing with the immediate instead of focusing on the long game.

- **R**ules: Meant to be guidelines and guard rails, they often become shackles and strongholds.

  You are embarking on a journey that will help you become a chain-breaker and, as a result, a wavemaker by discarding the rules that no longer serve you. At times, we adopt or accept these parameters for our safety or seasonal needs.

  We stop growing when we still honor them after they are no longer needed or necessary. It's like trying to wear a pair of shoes we've outgrown. They may have fit when we were younger, but they simply don't fit our needs now.

- **Attitudes:** The way we feel about something or someone.

  Our attitude about a situation, someone else, or even ourselves totally affects our feelings, actions, and energy. One of the few things we can truly control in our lives is our attitude. Is yours serving you or strangling you? Is it time to reassess what you think about your opportunities, opposition, and outcomes?

- **Perspectives:** What lens are you looking through when you look in the mirror or into the future?

  Now we see things imperfectly, like puzzling reflections in a mirror, but then we will see everything with perfect clarity. All that I know now is partial and incomplete, but then I will know everything completely, just as God now knows me completely. (1 Corinthians 13:2, NLT)

  The way we perceive things can completely block our ability to create. If we don't see ourselves as creators or creative, we have imperfect vision. Once we have the awareness, we can make changes.

My son played baseball when he was in the fourth grade. Two weeks in a row, he got hit in the face trying to catch a ball from the outfield during a night game. The second hit required a trip to the emergency room. It was then the doctor suggested he might need his vision checked.

After a trip to the eye doctor, we realized the boy needed glasses!

He never got hit in the face again and was a better player because he could see more clearly.

Is it time to get your vision checked regarding how you see yourself?

I'm willing to bet that when you were in preschool, you could take a blank page and a few crayons and use your imagination to create what, in your eyes, was magical.

That talent is still in you; it's simply been buried or diluted by life.

If you don't yet know of a woman named Amy Brooks, allow me to introduce you to her.

Amy is an author, artist, and motivational speaker. Sounds impressive and inspiring, right? It is. Especially in light of a condition she was born with called tetraphocomelia; Amy was born with no arms and no legs.

Amy didn't let the C.R.A.P. life gave her limit her possibilities. She got creative and has designed a life including her challenges. You can learn more about her through social media and her two-part book series, *Unseen Arms* and *Unseen Arms—Reaching Out*.

I caution you not to compare yourself to Amy. Apply her story as a conviction that God has something great in store for you. All you have to do is reach out for it.

As you begin to grow, change, and let go of what's no longer serving you, the people who are comfortable with the way you live will naturally become uncomfortable. Part of living in favor and as a force means, at times, letting people and things go. At a minimum, you may need to create some distance.

Your creative energy is going to be determined, in part, by those you associate with on a regular basis. Are you hanging around other creatives? Who in your life is also willing to make the necessary changes to design a life of permission, purpose, and passion as they pursue their calling?

You can do this through podcasts, books, and YouTube videos, even if you don't currently have personal contacts doing so. And here's a hint, the fact that you're reading this very book means you know four other women like yourself!

Don't get stuck in the weeds. Allow yourself to dream about all you can do and achieve. It's time to take imperfect action and create some epic stuff! It's time to Clear YOUR C.R.A.P. by breaking chains and making waves. I know. I've done it myself, and it's one of the most impactful processes I use with my clients.

## BECOME A FORCE—DAY 10

1. Get real. What is on your calendar that is causing chaos? Remember, it's *your* calendar, and if it's on there, you allow it. What can be delegated or dumped? Make a list of what you're going to release to let creativity take its spot.

2. Sometimes, rules are meant to be broken. What rules do you still honor because you've always done it that way? Is that rule still serving you? If not, you have permission to stop or alter it so it better suits you.

3. How do you let the attitudes of others affect you? Take some time to think about it. Who in your life is a naysayer? It's time to put on some protective armor and insulate your new awareness from them.

4. Now that you see things with a new perspective, how will you protect it and yourself when you're tempted to backslide or others try to pull you back into an old pattern?

# Day 11

## TIME

*She who trusts in the Lord will never be disappointed.*

—Isaiah 49:23 (NIV)

When you are truly ready to make changes, you know it. Your gut tells you, and your body knows even before your mind does. You get little sensations, nudges, and flashes of ideas. You may even start noticing signs or patterns that up until now you hadn't. Those little intuitions are really big insights into what you are being called to do.

I don't know about you, but waiting is not my favorite thing. I often think waiting is a waste of time, whether at a traffic light or in a waiting room—and don't get me started about being placed on hold with certain companies.

However, when I shift my perspective and recall a favorite saying of my Mimi's—good things come to those who wait—I am reminded of chocolate cake. (Hang with me; I've got a point.)

Whether you're a baker or simply enjoy baked goods, quality takes time. A chocolate cake cooked in a microwave is okay. However, made from scratch—sifted flour stirred with room temperature eggs and baked in an oven—it is definitely a better epicurean experience.

So it is with our goals and dreams. Some simply take longer and require more effort.

Since we can't control time nor can we get back what's already been used, we must master what we have. That applies to the hours in a day and the days left in our lives.

Now, I'm not judging anyone. I did not attend law school or pass the bar, nor do I own a gavel. And truth be told, I've binge-watched Netflix or spent too much time scrolling when I ought to have been using that time to get closer to a goal.

The key takeaway here is that when you are clear on your favor, you *want* to maximize your time. No one needs to nudge you or condemn you. Your internal drive is enough to guide you into making wise choices.

While we are on the subject of time, let's admit there is often no "perfect" time to begin or end something. My former mother-in-law had six children in a ten-year span. I'm fairly certain there was not a lot of calendar checking and budget consideration during that season of life. If they had stopped to ask if it was a good time to have another child, their family would have most likely wound up much smaller. They simply followed their hearts and passion.

If you have time-sucking commitments and people in your life, girlfriend, it may be hard to accept, but I dare suggest it's because you allow it. The one who controls your calendar is the one looking back at you from the mirror.

So, how can we maximize the time we have? The same 1440 minutes each of us has been gifted are ours to use or lose.

I imagine if you and I sat down to review your calendar and commitments, we'd be hard-pressed to add even one more thing. That's why it's important to be clear on your priorities. Because if we were to sit down face to face, I'd ask you how some things you're engaged in are actually propelling you toward your favor.

Know that I'm all for downtime, and we all need it. We call it reset or recovery time. Science has proven that time is necessary for you to grow and create the quality of life you deserve. Think about trees, flowers, and other plants. While they appear to be dormant during certain seasons, they're simply experiencing some time of refreshment, so they are prepared for their next season of growth.

So, what season are you in, friend? Are you actively growing? Are you making the time to replenish your supply? Remember, God created the world in only six days, and then he rested. Jesus often withdrew to rest and pray. Why do we think we don't deserve or need the same for ourselves? Our loved ones deserve it; our favor needs it. Living your best and fullest won't happen if you're always haggard.

Even one simple change can wind up making a tremendous difference. Have you heard of the butterfly effect?

It's the idea that something as small and seemingly insignificant as the flutter of a butterfly's wings can change the course of tornadoes and other storms.

Sister, are you in a storm right now?

What one tiny change can you make that could have a massive impact?

Here are a few of my favorite and most effective changes.

- Go to bed thirty minutes earlier each night for one week.

- Don't answer the phone unless it's one of your children or your spouse. Let all other calls go to voicemail. You can call them back when you have a free minute.

- Wake up thirty minutes earlier every morning for one week. If you combine that with an earlier bedtime, your entire day and energy shift.

- Meal plan and prep for one week.

- Lay out your clothes, skincare, and cosmetics the night before. In the morning, it's one less decision to make and one less thing to set up.

- Schedule time to breathe. I literally have six alarms set on my phone to remind me to breathe consciously and deeply throughout the day. If we're too busy even to breathe, we're too busy.

- Listen to podcasts or audiobooks while driving, working out, cleaning, or working in the kitchen.

As long as you allow others to determine your availability and accessibility, they control you. An *Unhackable Force* retains control, delegating and dumping what might slow them down.

When we stop sabotaging ourselves, our minds are clearer, our energy is increased, and our vision is sharper. It's easier to see and achieve what we want.

What is your gut telling you? What have you outgrown? What is not in alignment with your current dreams?

For some of us, being busy is comfortable. Always rushing and feeling under pressure is familiar. I've got some news for you; nothing new happens in our comfort zone. So whether you need to tighten up and dial in to intensify your focus or release and realign, is now a good time to do so?

## BECOME A FORCE—DAY 11

1. If you had a clear week with no commitments of any kind other than what you chose, what would stay on your calendar?

2. What would be taken off? What would you add?

3. To live in your favor, you'll need to set a deadline for your shift in activities. Don't let analysis paralysis kick in. Listen to your gut, assign a date for you to

start taking back your time, and write it in the space below. "Someday" is not a day of the week. Do it afraid.

This is the date I choose to claim my favor by taking back control of my time:

_____

## Permission Granted!

I choose to claim my favor by taking back control of my time.

Name _____

Signature _____

Date _____

For the record, it's okay to write in this book.

(Here's a last-minute tip. Make this date no longer than thirty days from today.)

# Day 12
## SPACE

*Having a clear mind and a clear space allows*
*you to think and act on purpose.*

—Erika Oppenheimer

The people, places, and possessions you surround your-self with have a direct impact on you. It may seem subtle or "normal" to you by now. However, what is the cost of being exposed and subject to those things? Remember the frog in the boiling water? Familiarity led to fatality.

Have you ever walked into a place that felt electric and the energy in the room was palpable? The colors, textures, light, and music all contributed to that feeling.

I bet you've also gone into other spaces and felt a different vibe. Maybe it was too much or too little of something? Perhaps it was the smell or overall feel that made you uncomfortable?

Our space, both physically and mentally, influences our ability to focus, produce, and even relax.

Why do spas have soft music and soothing colors? They're trying to evoke a serene atmosphere.

I remember when I first started working from home. I was so excited to be in control of my surroundings. I got to choose the music I listened to, what I wore, and where I sat—all well before 2020.

For my background sound, I chose to listen to classic rock, the stuff I listened to in high school. Without telling you my exact age, I will share it was AC/DC and Rush. By the end of my first few days working from home, I found myself short-tempered and easily agitated. I was worn out by the end of the day and generally not pleasant to be around.

What was the deal? I was in charge, and I thought that would make me happy and productive.

Then I realized the music I was listening to for eight hours a day was affecting me. It put me on edge to listen to the intensity and lyrics for so long. Once I changed the genre, I changed, and so did my productivity.

I'll still blast the old stuff now and again when I'm in speed-cleaning mode or going down the highway. However, my day-to-day creativity producing music, I've discovered, is classical.

Studies have actually shown that listening to music without lyrics and at medium energy will inspire—in other words, "happy" music versus anger-based. (My favorite tool is focusatwill.com. I signed up for a lifetime subscription, and it's been so helpful.)

Music isn't the only factor in living out your favor. The colors, lighting, smells, and textures in your space also play a role. Intentionally designing your ideal space will help your vision become a reality.

To quote Maria von Trapp, aka Julie Andrews, in the classic movie, *The Sound of Music*, "Let's start at the very beginning—a very good place to start."

Spend some time envisioning your most productive and enjoyable space.

Do you have lots of natural light? Do you prefer overhead lights or lamps?

Do you like soft colors, neutrals, rich colors, or brights?

Are the surfaces hard, soft, smooth, rough?

Do you work barefoot? If so, are your feet on carpet, tile, or hardwood floor?

Does your desk face a window? Is your back against a wall?

What color is the room? What kind of artwork adorns the walls?

Is there music, white noise, or no sound at all?

Do you work at a standing desk? In an oversized chair? An open desk or a classic roll-top?

I've had an in-home office for several years now. A couple of things are non-negotiable for me (and yes, I learned the hard way). My office is not in my bedroom because I need to be able to walk away. If that's not an option for you, can you put up a folding screen to create separation? Is there any extra space in a closet you can use to set up your office?

The other important thing for me is that household bills and papers are not kept with my business documents. I need to separate the two. Would you take your bills to an office outside your home? Most likely not. If space is an issue, a closed container or filing cabinet near your desk creates boundaries, so your finances and functions have some distance.

For today, I want you to spend a bit of time exploring and imagining. Set a time limit to scroll Pinterest, Houzz, or even peruse those magazines you've not been able to throw away. Remember, this is an assignment to expand, not numb out or distract yourself. I bet you'll be amazed at how quickly you can identify your desires. Setting a timer ensures you won't overthink or get lost in dreaming.

What draws you in? What makes you feel good, inspired, or excited by simply looking at it? If money were no object, how would you decorate your space? It's time to get a bit creative and indulgent. You might be surprised that what you find appealing and what you are currently surrounded by are very much alike or different.

## BECOME A FORCE—DAY 12

Today's task is simple and hopefully fun. Describe or draw your ideal space in the area below. If you can't envision your boon, begin by seeing your surroundings.

Dream it, see it, do it, create it, and realize it.

# DAY 13
## URGENCY

*I never dreamed about success. I worked for it.*

—Estee Lauder

Have you ever known someone who received a terminal diagnosis? Perhaps you've heard the Tim McGraw song, "Live Like You Were Dying."

Here's the bad news. Today is the youngest you'll ever be. If you're not going to take action now, when will you? Deadlines may come and go; however, your call or purpose in life never will.

If you knew the exact number of days you have left, what would you do with them?

Since most of us don't have any idea how much more time we'll be blessed with to fulfill our divine design or achieve the goals and dreams our soul longs for, if we don't start now, when will we?

If you're near the age of thirty or even well past it, you've had the opportunity to experience a high school reunion. Maybe a wedding is more relatable. Think of a big event where you want to look your best and lots of pictures will be taken.

That healthier lifestyle you've been putting off starting takes on a new sense of urgency. When the clock starts ticking, we tend to shift into high gear.

If you're a mom or have been around one with a newborn, how swiftly does she move into action when her child is crying or in harm's way?

A couple of days ago, you were encouraged to set a deadline or target for achieving your goal. I trust you did so, and now I ask, what's your sense of urgency?

Did you pick a "safe" date or one that would cause any real sense of drive or discomfort to kick in? Is your date a big enough desire?

Did you start the clock to generate changes in your current choices to reach your new level? Remember, work and distractions will expand to the amount of time we give them.

So, how can you create and maintain a sense of urgency? How can you stay pumped up, focused, and driven even when the struggles come your way?

One definition of urgency is insistence.

Have you ever dealt with a two-year-old who wants something NOW? You know the persistence, insistence, and need for immediate gratification she has.

Maybe by the time you read this book, you've been shushed or disappointed enough that you no longer have that sense of immediacy. The hassle and hustle may have worn you down.

My friend, all that can change right now.

A dream is a wish your heart makes. Even though life and others may disappoint you, declare this very moment that you can count on yourself. From this day forward, you will not let yourself down. When you make a commitment, stick to it, with the only exceptions being for something even grander or if you're in a harmful situation.

Pause for a minute and ask yourself what word urgency rhymes with. Did you figure it out?

Urgency rhymes with emergency.

We both know darn well and good that if you had an emergency, you would do whatever it took to save yourself, a loved one, or even a stranger.

Your favor, your purpose in life *is* in danger. It's a 911 call for your focus agency and your energy. We'll talk about those more in-depth over the next two days, but for now, it is imperative to create and maintain a laser-focused sense of completion. To do so, you need to protect yourself from things, including people, that will distract you or cause you to numb out.

When we are trying to avoid what we know we need to do, distractions are easily accessible. They allow us to feel busy and needed. Yet, are we truly being productive?

I've had many meals with someone who would take a bite or two of food then pick up their phone to play a game or check their status and updates on social media. If some people can't even eat a meal without tuning out, how can they accomplish a big goal?

While I'm on the subject of phones, how often do you touch yours? It's a great way to get lost in the urgent yet unimportant.

When you wake up in the morning—and I realize many women use their phones as alarm clocks like I do—what happens next? Do you check your social media feed or glance at your inbox before even getting out of bed?

Remember, I'm not judging. I simply want to increase your awareness of the slow fade that can occur from *I'm fired up and going for it,* to *well, it's not really that important.*

So, how can you establish a sense of urgency?

Being self-controlled and others-focused while reverse engineering your timeline is guaranteed to fan your flames and keep you going.

When we are truly in control of ourselves, we don't allow our emotions to decide or dictate our choices and actions.

Why do some women get up at 4:30 in the morning to get in a workout? Do they always want to? Trust me, that's a no. However, that same woman realizes that if she skips her exercise, she won't have the energy to complete her other tasks for the day, and she'll feel guilty and disappointed in herself. So, she does it anyway. Why? Because when she keeps her commitment to herself, she can serve others better—self-controlled and others-focused.

How about reverse engineering?

How did you decide on the date you set or are going to set to achieve your goal? Did you pick something based on another event or something random? Did you select a date and then work backward to break down the tasks into doable steps and shorter timelines?

The latter is reverse engineering, and some refer to it as starting with the end in mind. Either way, once the target has been established, it's easier to hit if we construct it backward.

## BECOME A FORCE—DAY 13

When it comes to urgency, it can feel like a lot of pressure because it's intense. So let's break it down into a two-part process.

**STEP 1**

What is your goal?

Who will it serve?

When will you achieve it?

How will you ensure completion or know when the work is complete?

Where will you need to make changes in your current commitments?

Why is it important to accomplish it?

## STEP 2

Often, we can become so focused we forget the joy. No joy means no urgency. Joy fuels urgency.

How will you celebrate?

What milestones will you celebrate along the way?

Now that you understand how crucial it is to fulfill your mission, you've got the fuel to make the necessary alterations to achieve it.

# DAY 14

## AGENCY

*Most people live and die with their music
still unplayed. They never dare to try.*

—Mary Kay Ash

Agency. It's not a word we often use outside advertising, modeling, employment, and a handful of other businesses. What about the business of your life? What if you decided to take agency over your choices?

Remember yesterday when we considered being self-controlled? It's another way to describe agency. The moment we decide to own our choices, we rise to a new level of awareness. We stop thinking or acting like a victim or the type of person life happens *to*.

Instead, we immediately become victors! *We* happen to life, and we embrace opportunities and give ourselves permission. We no longer allow circumstances and other people's limiting beliefs to inhibit us.

The word *decide* stems from the Latin words *de*, meaning off, and *caedere*, meaning cut. Once you decide, you've cut off other options.

Now that you have declared agency over your life, it's time to make more decisions. It's time to prune what no longer serves you. There will always be things you like to do. However, are they in your best interest? As we change, we need to evolve and transform. A former pastor of mine used the following example.

Imagine summertime. Picture a flowing sundress, fun flip flops, and broad-brimmed sun hat. It's perfect for the weather, and you enjoy being comfortable.

Now, picture yourself in that same attire in the middle of a snowstorm. You're not going to be comfortable, and in fact, you could be in danger of frostbite.

Life is like this example. Once you own your present and potential, changes are simply inevitable. You have a timeline and a sense of urgency. What do you need to adjust to make achieving your goals and enjoying your favor more feasible?

Little life hacks add up to big gains when they are implemented and maintained. Knowing and doing are two very different concepts. The word "know" has two meanings. In Greek, it refers to head knowledge. We know facts. We know right from wrong. We know what we ought to do.[16] However, in Hebrew, "know" means to be intimate or have a relationship with. Or, we could go so far as to say engaging.[17]

Look at it this way. We know lack of sleep will have detrimental effects on our health, but do we always get the rest we need? Do we employ in our lives what we know in our head? Does it make sense?

Delayed gratification, not something that many people honestly enjoy, is crucial to fully seize the opportunities before and within us.

Yes, you are the boss of yourself and can choose to do what you want. Is what you are choosing numbing or avoiding, or is it nudging and achieving? Consider it this way—delayed gratification equals long-term satisfaction.

For the record, I'm writing this text minutes before the deadline for edit. Why? Because I didn't practice enough what I preach! I gave into the immediate too often, and now, my back's up against the wall. I'm simply trying to keep it real.

There are times when we can pull an all-nighter or our productivity increases based on a tight deadline. Those instances need to be exceptions, not the rule. What are some ways you can create "agency?" What happens if or when you don't?

Creating agency will start first with a mindset enhancement. I invite you to consider an old phrase used when computers first came onto the consumer scene: Garbage in, garbage out.

Ultimately, you need to decide what is best for you. No one else ought to have that power. Yes, if you're in a committed relationship, it's a healthy and respectful discussion to have before you make major life changes. At the same time, someday you will be the one to answer for the accounting of your life and time. The only person blame and excuses serve is the one making them. How can you maximize your time?

If you're in a season of carpools and sports practices, how can you capitalize on that waiting time? It's a great time to return calls, review meeting notes, plan meals, or delete emails. For sports practices, how about using that time to get your exercise as well? Getting up early may not work for you; however, if your child is running up and down the field, how about taking a few laps around it? You can still watch your little one, and you're checking off something else from your list as opposed to adding another time commitment.

If you want to get creative with your schedule, I invite you to reach out to me (daphne@daphnevsmith.com). I've lived through seasons of childrearing, career climbing, studying as an adult student, and building a business as an entrepreneur. I bet that together we can create a calendar that works exactly how you need it to support your goals.

Now, let's look at the penalty part I mentioned.

If you've ever raised children, you know that sometimes a consequence needs to be given if a task has not been completed. For that matter, no children are required. If you have a job, you know there are penalties if you don't perform as expected.

What would it look like if you held yourself to the same level of accountability? When I was in direct sales many years ago, I had the privilege of being trained by the legendary Mary Kay Ash. Her teachings, philosophy, and ethics were inspiring. I remember one training session when she proposed the question, "Why wouldn't you work as hard for yourself as you would someone else?" That's both sobering and encouraging.

What penalty will you pay if you don't follow through on your goal commitments? Again, it's entirely up to you. You get to have agency over yourself. It's not my job or anyone else's to force you to achieve. The choice is entirely up to you. Will you choose life or death for your boon?

## BECOME A FORCE—DAY 14

Your boon is helpful or beneficial. It makes sense to want to achieve it, so what happens if you don't?

Now's the time to commit to a consequence. Remember, it has to have significance for you. If you're money-motivated, then perhaps if you miss a deadline, you can write a check to an organization you don't agree with or support for an amount that makes you cringe.

If you're food-motivated, perhaps you forego a particular treat or daily enjoyment of something for thirty days—think chocolate or coffee.

What motivates *you*? The penalty you choose must have meaning. Once you've decided on it, it's time to share it with someone who will hold you accountable.

What's your penalty?

Who will you tell?

When will you begin?

# DAY 15

## ENERGY

*The truth is, it's not about willpower;*
*it's about reducing decisions.*

—Robyn Conley Downs

No supplement drinks are needed—your energy increases when you are laser-focused, clear in your calling, and inspired by your intention. These elements combined create an alignment with your true source for everything you will ever need.

There's no need to stay stuck, frustrated, defeated, or overwhelmed. You CAN break the chains keeping you personally and professionally restricted. Once you do, you'll start making waves!

Sometimes, we simply need to give ourselves permission to go for it! I have your permission slip waiting for you. Are you ready to claim it? If so, let's go!

Everything is energy. It is simply and yet complexly the capacity for doing work. Whether the energy is potential, kinetic, thermal, electrical, chemical, nuclear, or other various forms, it is used to create. Harnessing your energy will dictate where you put your attention.

Studies prove that women are more efficient than men. We use our energy differently, and while that often serves us, it can also be detrimental.

If you are lacking energy, are you leaking it? Energy is renewable; your time is not. Let's check your energy distribution. When your phone or computer has too many open tabs, it can't perform at its maximum capacity. We think it does; after all, look at all that is happening at the same time. The truth is, having all those open tabs slows down processing. How many mental tabs do you have open?

A sign you are overtaxed is if you feel or use these words to describe yourself:

- tired
- overwhelmed
- burned out
- running on empty
- fried
- toasted
- drained
- exhausted
- freaking out
- agitated

Decision fatigue is a big contributor to all of these feelings. It's estimated that as adults, we make over 35,000 remotely-conscious decisions every day. Not to add pressure, but each of those has a consequence. Now, don't jump to analysis paralysis. Breathe!

You are not consciously aware you're making many of those decisions. It doesn't mean they don't still require energy. It does mean that efficiency with decisions and establishing systems will help conserve your energy. Life isn't always about doing more; it's about allocating energy where it is most needed.

Over the last few days, I've shared some tips and hacks to get you thinking about today. If you've ever worked in a retail environment, you may remember inventory time. During one season of my life, I worked for a department store managing a cosmetic counter. I remember the first time we conducted overnight inventory. Have you ever stopped to think about how small eyeshadows and lipsticks are? When it comes time to count hundreds of them, you become aware.

While inventory may not always be something to anticipate with delight, the results are necessary. If we aren't aware of our actual resources and, in this case, energy drains, we can easily run out of what we need to carry out our mission.

The first place to begin is your calendar, which is a reflection of your commitments and priorities. It reveals what you truly value because if it matters, it needs to be scheduled. Would you ever just pop into your OB/GYN for an exam or drop by your hairdresser, hoping she could see you on a whim?

When you review your schedule, are there some things that can be delegated or totally eliminated? Not everything in life can have the same priority.

*Tip: If you're using multiple calendars, merging them will save time, overlap, and missed appointments. Also, be sure to record promises. If you've ever accidentally stood someone up, forgotten to pick up a child, or missed a deadline, most likely, it wasn't on your calendar.

Next, let's consider time-saving tools. Several years ago, when they first came out on the market, my best friend invested in a remote robotic vacuum cleaner, and I thought she was absurd. Today, I see the genius behind saving time while accomplishing a goal—cleanliness.

Because of our achievements and accomplishments, we all have increased duties and responsibilities. Using our time wisely honors them.

Do you currently use the auto-brew feature on your coffee maker? How about auto-pay for your bills? Need to renew your car tag? Try doing so online. Are you grocery shopping or picking up?

*Tip: Tools and services are provided to maximize your choices and efficiency. They are intended to free you to enjoy the things you love or carry out the tasks only you can do.

Every time you say "yes" or agree to something, you say "no" to something else by default. If you live in a state of constant apologizing, guilt, or running late, it's time to exercise your "no" more often.

In my favorite book, a passage helps me remember that saying yes to everyone and everything does not serve anyone well. Am I now trying to win the approval of human beings or God? Or am I trying to please people? If I were still trying to please people, I would not be a servant of Christ. (Galatians 1:10 NIV)

The bottom line is you can't and won't make everyone happy. If you're going to disappoint someone, don't let it be yourself.

When you set up systems to streamline decisions and conserve energy, your choices are easier to make. If you're feeling confused and overwhelmed, you might be leaking. The world is full of distractions disguised as opportunities. When you are clear on your passion and purpose, you automatically give yourself permission to say no to certain things because they simply aren't a match for this season in your life.

The good news is that can change right now, today. It starts with a small step, followed by another and another.

## BECOME A FORCE—DAY 15

Practice and prepare your "no," recognizing that single word as a complete sentence. You don't owe anyone an explanation.

With that in mind, what are you pre-deciding to say "no" to the next time you receive a request?

It doesn't have to be major. A simple, easy one might be the best place to start.

Make a list of your top three no's. By doing so now, you won't have to decide later. You'll be prepared, and I promise you, it will be even just a tiny bit easier.

1.

2.

3.

# PART 3

# Unhackable Reach

# DAY 16

## STUCK SHOULD BE A FOUR LETTER WORD!

*You can't reach for anything new if your
hands are still full of yesterday's junk.*

—Louise Smith

Welcome to our journey through *Unhackable Force*! I am excited to spend Days 16 through 22 with you. This section is called Unhackable Reach. Working through it, you will truly understand how to reach new stages in your life with your God-given passion and have a bigger reach with your message.

You have worked through the first two sections with Debra and Daphne, so you are at the halfway point, rounding second base, and on the stretch to third. (We are a big sports family, and I always find myself using sports analogies, so just go with it lol.)

Why me for this week? Well, two words people use to describe me are Encourager and Elevator. I love to encourage, motivate, and empower people to reach their next level, to live a life with passion and do what makes their heart happy, and to step in with their story and share it with the world.

Now, I always knew I was an encourager, but one day, I had some very important people in my life tell me my word was "Elevator."

I started thinking, why the heck am I an elevator? Yes, I was thinking of an actual elevator, one that takes you up and down floors of a hotel or other building! I thought to myself, why on earth, with all the words they could give me, did they pick the word elevator? It took me a moment to wrap my head around it, but once they described it, its definition, and why they gave it to me, I owned it. Yes, I am an Encourager and an Elevator! Do you have a word or two that describe you? I bet you do.

My goal in the next seven days is to encourage and elevate you to a life of passion and purpose. Through many years of working with women of all ages, one word comes up time and time and time and time again. (Yes, I used it four times for effect.) Women always tell me they feel **stuck**!

Let's refer back to this day's title: Stuck Should Be a Four Letter Word. Think about it: Stuck in traffic, stuck in a bad relationship, stuck at the airport, stuck in a job you hate, feeling stuck in your life—it all makes you feel like you want to yell a four-letter word. Am I right?

So let's rethink the word "stuck." You're not stuck—you are in transition—transitioning from where you are now to the next stage. Sometimes we don't know how to get from point A to point B (and sometimes we don't even know point A), but this is where we have to do the work, go deep, and, more importantly, enjoy the journey.

We get frustrated when we see where we want to go, and we either:

- Don't know how to get there

- Are kept from getting there by something

- Are simply overwhelmed

- Don't believe that we can do it.

This is when you feel stuck. You need to start thinking of this as a transition. How you handle that transition and the energy you put into it is the difference between feeling stuck, overwhelmed, sad, or hopeless and feeling excited about where the next journey will take you.

Stuck is when you are being hacked. We feel purposeless and unproductive. It's not a good place to live.

Transition is where we learn to become Unhackable. Choosing a life of passion and purpose requires focus. I love helping others achieve this focus by thinking about their pain—their stuckness—and embracing it rather than ignoring it or wallowing in it. It's part of your story—your journey. By owning your pain, you eliminate the risk of losing sight of your path while focusing on someone else's.

Women especially are focused on everyone else's dreams: what we need to do to help our kids get to the next level and what we need to do for our jobs, spouse, or home. Then we can get lost in social media and wish we had someone else's life. Online photos of friends or influencers cause feelings of jealousy as you see others' success and instantly become envious. Our focus can quickly shift from ourselves to others as we keep track of their wonderful lives and lose track of our actual assets. The list goes on and on.

I know you can relate in one way or another. It's the "grass is always greener" scenario. Social media and the internet are a million times worse because we have access to billions of backyards—and those backyards hack us!

We need to get to the next level by discovering our true passion, what we were designed and put on this earth to do. Let me say that it's in you. Don't think it's not! Unhackability means

- Aligning with your passion.

- Focusing on yourself instead of comparing yourself to others and what they are doing.

- Redirecting your focus.

Only then can you close that gap between you and your God-given story that's waiting for you.

I know some of you are thinking, "*I don't even know what that is anymore.*" I've been there many times in my life! But here's the thing; it is in you! You have to dive deep and do the work so that it resurfaces.

It's kind of like when you hear a song on the radio that you haven't heard in twenty years. You used to love the song, but you've totally forgotten about it! But when that song comes on, you sing every single word like you are Mariah Carey! You love it, and it means something to you or brings back memories. *The song is in you.* You may not have thought about it for twenty years, and it hasn't come into your mind in forever, but the minute you hear it, you sing along and know every single word.

That is like your dream, your God-given passion, and what you are meant to do with your life. I promise it's in you.

It may sound strange, but many times it's our pain and what we've been through that is our story. That is how we help others, create our dream for a business, travel, or whatever it is. That dream is in us, but we have done such a great job of stuffing it down, ignoring it, and telling ourselves reasons why it won't ever happen that we eventually forget about it.

So, remember when I touched on my story about finding my passion and heart when I was competing for the Mrs. International title? Before then, I was like a lot of you. I was working; I had two little girls, a husband, and a house, and everything seemed great! The only thing is I felt stuck!

I felt like there was something more for me, something else out there I was supposed to do with a deeper meaning.

Now, what you don't know is that at the time, I had been significantly involved with the American Diabetes Association.

When I met my husband, he told me that at age seventeen, he was diagnosed with juvenile diabetes, or what today we call Type 1 diabetes. When I knew he would become a permanent part of my life, I knew his diabetes would too. I studied and learned everything I could about the disease. I felt as if I had a degree in diabetes education (okay, so not a real degree, but I knew a lot)!

When my girls were young, I went to the library to find a children's book about diabetes and what to do if mommy wasn't home and daddy needed help. Yes, years ago, you had to go to the library and go through the card catalog to find information. I know; I am showing my age, and many of you reading this will have no idea what I am talking about.

Well, there was nothing I could find about the subject. So, I went home and took it upon myself to write a children's book for my girls. You see, I knew there were millions of Americans with loved ones with diabetes who don't fully understand it and how to help someone with this disease. I needed to get out and share my message and what I've learned with other people who needed it. It was in my heart, and I knew it, but I was thinking, *how am I going to do this? Who's going to listen to me; I'm just one person.* Then, of course, when you talk to others, they can be a little less enthusiastic and say things like, "*Oh, that's nice*" or "*How in the world are you ever going to make that happen?*"

You see, nobody sees the dream as you do, and people aren't going to buy into a vision they don't understand. You're going to have those people who are naysayers, or who poo-poo on your dream, or who blow it off. That is where you truly have to become Unhackable! You need to align with all the things you have, that story deep inside you know will help others, and you are called to share. Everybody's deep passion is there, but we have to be in that transitioning place and know where we're headed, and we can redirect all that energy and passion to our God-given story!

## THIS IS WHERE WE BEGIN TO DREAM BIGGER!

Every dream, passion, or boon (pick whichever word resonates with you) will attract its share of critics and cynics. If it doesn't, it's probably too safe or too small. You see, you can't control what others say about you or your dream, but you can control how you respond. Engaging with haters only hacks you, and you lose focus by letting them inside your head and heart. You exchange creating for combatting. If your goal is to prove you're right, you'll give away your power. However, if your goal is to achieve your dream, you can maintain your power by letting this fight strengthen your posture.

Maybe this will help. Imagine if I had a cool gift for one of my kids that I absolutely knew they were going to love. I know my kids better than anyone, and I know what gets them fired up and excited. If I told my kids, *I have a gift for you, and I promise you will love it*, they would be excited, expectant, and waiting for their gifts. With this gift called life and all the things God wants to give us, for some reason, we lose that joy, that excitement, that thrill of what's next, and what gift He will be sharing with us next.

Hold on to the excitement and expectancy of what you're called to do and how exciting that next stage can be. As I'm writing this, I feel a little stuck in a transition. It's a long story, but the Spark Notes version is my husband got a new job, they are relocating us back to where we originally lived, and I couldn't be more excited. We have a new granddaughter who lives closer to where we will be moving, and I am super excited to get there, but we are in a crazy housing market right now.

We have been looking for several months, and we have yet to find a house. So, I sit and get frustrated, wondering why we are stuck here, but then I think of it instead as a transition.

I get up every morning, expectantly waiting for that house I know is ours to come up on the real estate page. Only yesterday, we thought we found one, but it sold before we could even get there to see it. Was I disappointed? Heck yes! It was in a perfect area, and I liked it okay, but if I'm being honest, it didn't check off many of my boxes.

I was settling because what I want to happen and what God has for us isn't lining up. My faith was a little off, but then I thought of my message about what I believe in this journey—that God has the best gift waiting, and I simply need to await it. I can't wait to be able to share the end of this story with you as I am sure it will make it into one of my talks. I know it will be exactly what we needed, even though this transition can be challenging.

People get a lot of this wrong. They merely sit back and wait, and when things aren't progressing, or they get frustrated, the feeling of being stuck sets in. We have to keep moving, do our part, dive deep, and figure out our next best step. I am working on how I can be prepared to move when the gift presents itself!

That is what I want for you. I want you to be able to move from feeling stuck in your life, like you don't know what the next move is, and you feel paralyzed. You want to do more or accomplish more; you know there is that thing you want to do, big or small, but you feel paralyzed. You feel stuck, and you don't know what your next step is. I want you to discover what will help transition you to that next S.T.A.G.E. in life. So, let's dive in and discover what that is for you. Let's find out what you want to set your sights on!

## BECOME A FORCE—DAY 16

There are so many stuck stories I could share about the many times in my life when I have felt stuck. When I replaced the word *stuck* with the word *transition* in my mind, I discovered what I'm going to walk you through—The S.T.A.G.E. Process. That made it easier, and I could move through it, expecting I was in transition to a new S.T.A.G.E.

Write down all the places you feel stuck. Don't hold back; dump them all. I want you to see on paper what is hacking you, holding you back, and keeping you from your next best stage in life.

# DAY 17
## SET YOUR SIGHTS

*You don't get what you want; you get who you are.*
*And who you are is a direct result of your focus.*

—Kary Oberbrunner

I love the above quote. What we choose to focus on is so powerful. The opinion we have of ourselves is the opinion that matters the most.

Stop focusing on what everybody else is doing or wishing for a better future, and start focusing on what's already all around you. I believe your God-given purpose is already inside you. Open your mind's eye, and you'll see everything you need.

For the next five days, I'm going to walk you through The S.T.A.G.E Process so that whenever you feel like you're transitioning to a new stage in life, you can go back and apply it to your new situation.

Let's begin the S.T.A.G.E. process with **Setting Your Sights**. For some of you, this is a no-brainer, and you already have your sights set on exactly where you're moving and the outcome you want. For others, it's buried so deep inside that it's going to take work to get it into the forefront of your world.

As women, we are constantly evolving, coming up with new and exciting ideas, and that's what makes life fantastic! Sometimes life comes at us, and we feel overwhelmed, confused, sad, lonely. I could go on and on, but I'll stop there. When we start embracing the transitioning phases of our life and looking at them as gifts, life takes on an exciting new meaning.

## LIFE ISN'T HAPPENING TO US; IT'S HAPPENING FOR US!

When I'm working with women, I get asked this question all the time: *Do dreams, goals, or setting your intentions for something have to be really big? Do they have to wow people?*

The answer to that is *no*! They don't have to wow anybody except you! They have to give you joy and get you excited every day to start your new journey, whatever that may be. It doesn't have to be something like, *I want to build a $2 million home, start a brand new business*, or *go back to college to get a degree to be a doctor.*

Maybe you love science, cooking, writing blogs, doing videos, or championing causes. Whatever it is, figure out what gets you excited and what you have a love and passion for.

I want to share a story about a client of mine who I worked with several years ago. She was kind of in that transition place we all get. She was feeling directionless, and she didn't know what she wanted to do. She was in a job she wasn't crazy about, and she needed something to get her excited to get out of bed every day. She needed something to look forward to, something that spoke to her heart and she had a passion for. I'm sure some of you out here can relate. I know I can.

So, when I started asking questions, and we began to talk about it, I found out she had always wanted to take her dog to agility classes—you know, those crazy courses where dogs go through an obstacle course. They run through tunnels, cross over bridges, jump over bars, and do all kinds of things while being timed. She thought it would be so much fun, and it was always in the back of her mind. So we talked about it, and I could hear the excitement and passion in her voice for the first time in our conversation.

When I challenged her to start taking action steps on what the process might look like if she signed up for a class, she gave me all the reasons it wouldn't work.

- Too much time

- Too expensive

- Too frivolous for a goal and purpose

- Too old to start something new

I challenged her to do it anyway!

To make a long story short, she signed up for her first class with her dog. She achieved that small goal she thought was a tiny little thing, something she could start with. You know the way you feel when it seems you're going to start with only a baby step; it was nothing big that turned into her passion and love.

Here we are several years later, and I see Facebook posts all the time on how she is traveling all over the United States with her two dogs, doing agility trials, and winning awards. The best part is she is meeting amazing people and has a whole different life than she had several years ago. She was in that stuck place but took an action step, stepped out of her comfort zone, and found a whole new life open to her.

Now, I'm not going to say we didn't have to work through self-doubt and opposition. She let her mind tell her about why it wouldn't work and how she didn't have time. There were so many things she came up with, but because it was her passion and love, she found out how to make it work. She didn't know where that little dream, that seed in her, would take her. I always tell people,

> *Your seed, that little passion that you have,*
> *it's all you need if God is your gardener. He*
> *takes that passion, that purpose, and your*
> *story and makes it into a wonderful thing.*

If it brings you joy and happiness, no matter what it is—a dog class, a cooking class, going back to school to become a doctor, writing a book, sharing your message on a stage with the world, or whatever your heart beats for—the most important thing you are going to learn through this week is that if you don't have a true passion for what you're doing, success is going to be much more difficult to achieve.

With passion and purpose for what you're doing, you've got what it takes, and you only need to take the next best step.

So I hope this helps you think about where you want to go on your next journey. Like I said earlier, I believe your God-given purpose is already inside you. Open up your mind's eye, and you'll see everything you need.

## BECOME A FORCE—DAY 17

I can hear some of you saying now, "I don't even know what to set my sights on!" You're not entirely sure what your dream lifestyle looks like; you simply know you are ready for a change. I get it; I have been there many times in my life. I understand the frustration you may be feeling.

When we feel stuck or lack excitement about our lives, sometimes it takes some focus to get us on the right path.

The following questions are designed to help you understand what moves you so you can set out to discover your best life. You can live your passion, but only if you find the courage to create it. To access 10 QUESTIONS TO HELP YOU DISCOVER YOUR PASSION and a Free 3 DAY BONUS go to UnhackableForce.com

## TEN QUESTIONS TO HELP YOU DISCOVER YOUR DREAM

Ask yourself these questions and figure out what your heart truly beats for because no one can steer you in the right direction except you. Your dream is worth fighting for, so **Set Your Sights** on it, and you will be on the road to your new S.T.A.G.E. in life.

1. What do you like to do in your free time?

2. What do people always tell you you're good at?

3. What would you like to learn with no intention of having it as a business?

4. What did you enjoy as a child?

5. Who are the three people you admire the most, and what do you admire about them?

6. What were you good at as a child?

7. What skills are you most drawn and attracted to?

8. What is your hobby?

9. What would you do even if you didn't get paid to do it?

10. What would you like to be doing if money and time were not an issue?

# DAY 18

## TRANSITION YOUR THOUGHTS

*Change your thoughts and you change your world.*

—Norman Vincent Peale

N ow it's time to move to the **T** in the S.T.A.G.E Process, and that, my friend, will be one people will work on throughout their lives. We're going to do some real soul searching here and really hit this one hard. I want you to get this concept so deeply inside of yourself that you are equipped to handle whatever negative thoughts your mind can conjure and all the decisions running through your mind. Here's my advice:

- Don't let your mind bully you.

- Close all the unopened windows. (I promise this step will make sense at the end of this day.)

If I could tell my younger self one thing of importance about this subject, it would be to understand that you cannot live peacefully in your body if your mind is constantly at war with you. You see, how you talk to yourself is a powerful thing and can keep you from making decisions. Too many choices running around in your mind will always hack you, and you will struggle with making these decisions. That often results in feeling stuck and unable to move forward with your passion and purpose. As a result, you can easily slip into overwhelm and confusion which holds you back even more. I am so passionate about helping women transition their thoughts; it's incredibly powerful!

To begin *transitioning your thoughts*, we first must clear space for a clearer vision and path for where you're going. Sometimes our minds can be like an overloaded computer, with too many things running in the background. Who can relate to that? I know if my office, desk, or kitchen is a mess, or if there is any mess at all, it brings stress and anxiety to me when I'm looking at it. Can I get an amen?

Organization and order help me feel more peaceful and ready for the day. The truth is that our minds get overwhelmed with all the chaos and unfinished "open windows" we have. In the original *Unhackable* book, Kary Oberbrunner tells the reader to do a Google image search with *too many browser tabs*. The image results could push someone over the edge, especially if you're the person trying to keep track of all the open windows on the computer. That's how we can feel with too many things going on and running in the background of our minds.

Your computer feels the same way, and all those activities sabotage productivity. Every computer has a limited amount of RAM; if too many things are opened and going on at once, the computer's performance is severely hacked. There are so many reasons our computers are slow, and ironically, many of these reasons hack us too. I'm going to list a few reasons our computers might be slow, and let's see if there are any parallels to why **you** might be running slow:

1. You have too many startup programs going.

2. Your hard drive is failing.

3. Your hard drive is 95 percent full.

4. Your browser has too many add-ons.

5. You are running too many programs at once.

6. You have too many browser tabs open.

The computer is trying to do too many things at once. Sound familiar? Look, when I tweak the word and say "you," those six things are what we're feeling as well. I relate most to number 5—*You are running too many programs at once!*

Yep, that's me—too many things going on at once. I bet you all can relate as well. Then add your mind bullying you and telling you you're not accomplishing things; you're "not enough" to do all the things you need to do, or you're drowning because you're not good at what you do. It's no wonder we have no time for our passions and dreams or to step into our own true story!

Although humans are different from computers, in some ways, we're not. We may not consciously think of all the tasks we need to do, the places we need to go, and the people we need to see, but this is definitely going on in our subconscious.

In *Unhackable*, Kary Oberbrunner calls these things "Open Windows." We can't move on with our passion and dreams with all of these open windows. That's when we feel empty, stuck, and spread too thin before we even start; that is when our impact truly suffers!

Hacked people rarely make decisions. As a result, they leave many windows open. Indecision requires that our subconscious keep expending energy and attention on unresolved issues. As with a computer, these open windows drastically reduce our overall performance and productivity. Open windows hack our focus by introducing an endless number of distractions.

Decisions are powerful because they signify closure. Closure is permanent and helps you move forward. So when we make a decision, we are letting go of the other options available to us and taking up our brainpower; thus, we remain open to other possibilities in the future. We fail to realize not making a decision is actually a decision itself. By choosing not to decide, we are choosing to stay exactly where we are.

Indecision doesn't solve a problem, and it only prolongs the pain. So, let's get that hard drive cleaned up! It is time to do some decision making, so let's use the *Unhackable Impact Equation*.

## BECOME A FORCE—DAY 18

# UNHACKABLE IMPACT EQUATION©

DO IT ⟶ *You do it!*

DELEGATE IT ⟶ *Somebody else does it!*

DUMP IT ⟶ *Nobody does it!*

DECIDED = CLOSED WINDOW → AMPLIFY IMPACT

DELAY IT ⟶ *Who does it?*

UNDECIDED = OPEN WINDOW → INHIBIT IMPACT

Let's discuss the four-part process called **Closed Windows.** That helps clear up headspace for all the decisions we need to address and take charge of to get our power back!

**1. Identify**. Using a piece of paper or sticky note, write down your unresolved issues. These are all the undecided issues running in the background of your mind. Don't rush the process.

If you give yourself a few minutes, they will keep coming to the surface. They could be big or small. Write them all down:

- Organize kitchen
- Laundry
- Make dentist appointments
- Cancel appointment for dog
- Mow lawn
- Write a book
- Order products for my business
- Start working on a new business
- Shop for groceries
- Take dog to vet
- Finish college
- Change career

It doesn't matter how small or how big, but write down everything running in the back of your mind. When I started doing this, I had a ton of post-it notes, each with an open window running in my head. Now I work hard at doing this exercise every day so I can feel less stress about the day ahead.

**2. Arrange.** Look at the open windows, and spread them out on the table or wall. Do you realize they are hacking you? Do you know, subconsciously, you are spending an incredible amount of attention and energy trying to deal with these issues?

**3. Decide.** If you want to step into your passion and have a better impact, you need to close some windows. You need to decide to put these notes in one of three categories:

**4. Delay.** If there's one decision too important to decide, consider delaying it for 72 hours. Only do this for one open window if you **absolutely must**, and only do it if your head and heart conflict. Otherwise, decide to close all the windows now.

- **Do It**: This is where you decide you need to do the thing! Take care of it yourself, and get it off your plate.

- **Delegate It**: Give this to someone else. There are so many things we think only we can do, but I promise if you start delegating tasks (or hire them out if you can) and decide to let go of the stress, it will free up so much mind space!

- **Dump It**: Decide this is not of true importance, and it's time to let it go.

It's time to start transforming your thoughts. Stop bullying yourself, and move toward making decisions that will impact your passion and dream.

# DAY 19
## ACTIVATE YOUR PASSION

*Follow your passion; it will lead to your purpose.*

—Oprah Winfrey

Are you ready to learn the **A** in The S.T.A.G.E. Process? You have **Set Your Sights**, you're working hard to clear up the space to **Transform Your Thoughts,** and now you're going to **Activate Your Passion** and align yourself with people who can help you along your journey to accomplish what you're setting your sights on. (I call these people my Impact Crew, and we will dive in deeper on why it is so important to surround yourself with the right kind of company of friends.)

Focusing on *your* purpose requires you to go all-in with your God-given passion and identity and, more importantly, believe you are enough to do it. Whether you know it or not, you are changing in several ways, the most significant being:

**We don't see things as they are; we see them as we are. —Anaïs Nin**

Remember, self-image affects everything. It influences the way we see our story and calling. The truth is, we don't get what we want out of life; we get who we are. Knowing that changes everything.

For those who don't know my story or haven't read my book, *Miss Conception,* I struggled with a negative body image in my late teens and early twenties. I had low self-esteem, and negative self-talk was a huge part of my life when my battle with body negativity began at around eighteen.

I remember my mind started telling me my body wasn't perfect and that something was wrong with me. The way I looked wasn't the ideal I thought everyone expected of me or what I saw in magazines or television. My mind started playing tricks with me when I looked in the mirror. I'm sure many of you can relate. To this day, I look back at pictures of when I was young, and I wonder what the heck I was so unhappy about!

## HOW YOU SEE YOURSELF = YOUR IDENTITY

I constantly bullied myself and filled myself with negative self-talk. I would look in the mirror and focus on the imperfections I thought I saw. I would stay away from social situations because it usually required going out to eat, and I always felt like I lost control; that was so important for me to maintain. There were so many "not enough" feelings. I used to keep a journal and write down how I was feeling. I would write down all the negative things my mind said, and I believed. I did that every day.

I constantly fed my mind and gave energy to all my negative feelings. When friends would ask me to go out, those feelings controlled my decisions. I think about that to this day, and it truly brings tears to my eyes. It was tremendously difficult to be in my early twenties and not enjoy the magical life before me because of how my mind bullied me. I put all my energy into those feelings.

You see, our minds can be our biggest enemies, and when we start feeding our thoughts more and more negative information, we start believing it. We get dissatisfied, critical, sad, depressed, and we lose our joy. I lived the majority of my younger life lacking joy, joy that was taken from me by me because of how I saw myself. All my decisions would be made around how I felt about myself and my lack of confidence or feelings of "not enough."

Indecision requires our subconscious to keep expending energy, and that drastically reduces our overall performance and productivity. By transitioning our thoughts to necessary decision-making, we create a new space for our God-given story.

So no matter your age, if I could tell you one thing, it's this—

## DON'T LET YOUR MIND BULLY YOU!

We have enough against us with the bombardment of:

- Social media pictures

- Photos and magazines

- Models

- Commercials

- TV personalities and entertainers

Those all tell us how to think and act, what's important, and what it means to be happy or successful. It's no wonder we second-guess ourselves when we have a passion or goal or want to do something. We look at everyone else, and we think, *can I be as good as so and so? Do I have enough? Do I have what* *it takes? I don't look like*_____ *(fill in the blank).* We bombard ourselves every day with negative self-talk.

It's time to stop the madness! How do we begin to stop letting our minds bully us and start believing we're amazing? Well, it all starts with our belief system. For me, it came down to self-talk. It came down to changing my belief system about seeing myself and not focusing on what I thought I didn't have. Instead, I was determined to focus on what I did. Once I started doing that and feeling better and speaking more positively about myself, my confidence rose. Then I made those decisions I needed to make to move forward.

So, let's start with self-talk. What do you say to yourself when you get up in the morning and look in the mirror? What do you say to yourself when you're simply not feeling equipped to do something you set your mind to do? What do you say to yourself when you don't feel like you're enough?

We are really good at tearing ourselves down when someone else even compliments us. I see this all the time, especially with women. If friends compliment us, we have a hard time simply saying *thank you.* Women especially tend to want to negate positives toward them by others.

For instance, you probably recognize this exchange:

*"You look really great in those jeans. I love them."*
"Oh no, these jeans make me look so fat."

You've likely been on both sides of this exchange:

*"You look pretty today. I like the way you did your makeup."*
"Are you kidding me? I didn't do my makeup very well this morning, and gosh, I need to get a haircut."

You even put down your hair, and it was never even mentioned. You make sure people see how awful you feel. We have gotten to a place where we are uncomfortable with accepting a compliment from anyone. The more we focus on something, the bigger it gets in our minds, and then we get really good at bullying ourselves.

Most of us tend to stay in that negative space and go down a road of self-destruction. I say self-destruction because that is exactly what it is. When you listen to the thoughts that come into your head, you give them energy, and you go down that "not enough" path. You tear down everything you have tried to build up.

We have got to stop the cycle. We have got to learn not only to build each other up but, more importantly, we have got to learn to build ourselves up. It has to start within us.

The hard part about self-talk is that it always feels true. Even though your negative thoughts are incorrect, you choose to assume they're facts. Here is some great news; you can learn to notice your negative self-talk as it happens and choose to think more positively. It's going to take some time to practice, but it will be worth it. Believe me, once you start focusing on what you're saying, you will be surprised at how much your thinking is exaggerated or focused on the negative.

Our thoughts inspire our actions. So, if we can begin to change how we think, we begin to change how we feel and act.

This is going to take some work, especially if you have a long history of negative self-talk. It didn't begin overnight, so it's definitely not going to change overnight. I'm going to give you some steps to start you on your way to positive self-talk so you can begin to activate your passion.

## BECOME A FORCE—DAY 19

**1.** I want you to envision what it's like to be a confident you. This is a great exercise. I want you to start by creating an image of yourself as the confident, self-assured person you aspire to become. Now think about how it feels to be that person, how others will look at you, what your body language looks like, and how you come across to others.

I want you to close your eyes and really see this clearly in your mind. Practice doing this exercise every morning. How will you show up in your day, and what would it look like to show up certain of yourself and exude that kind of energy? It's going to take practice to be something you consciously think about all day. Soon you will show up as you see yourself more and more.

I still practice this if I'm going to be in a situation where I know I will be uncomfortable and uneasy. I get into this positive headspace, and I walk into that room confident in who I am. The opinion you have of yourself is the most important opinion you hold, and you constantly convey what you're feeling on the inside.

If you feel unattractive on the inside, you can be the most beautiful person in the world but convey feelings of unattractiveness, and it will push people away.

You see, the problem is on the inside. You carry yourself the way you see yourself, so what's on the inside eventually shows up on the outside.

**News Flash!** *People tend to see you the way you see you. You carry yourself the way you see yourself.*

**2.** Don't compare yourself to others. It's easy to measure your worth against other people; I get it. But find what you're good at, and keep your focus on yourself, not others. You will always find someone who has accomplished something you wish you could or has something you wish you had.

If you constantly compare yourself to others, you will always be on the losing end of that equation. Begin embracing your uniqueness and your accomplishments. Start creating your own goals and personal development plan, work towards being the best version of yourself, and stop worrying about everyone else.

**3.** Positive reinforcement: Stop building negative thoughts upon negative thoughts; it's time to start telling yourself some positive affirmations. Start small with very focused statements. They don't have to be big and elaborate. Say them out loud to yourself. Some examples are

- I am enough.
- I am healthy and happy.
- I am more than my appearance.
- I am a good person.
- I am loved.
- I am loyal.
- I am happy.
- I am healthy.
- I can do anything I put my mind to.
- I love myself.

The list could go on endlessly; pick a few that resonate with you, and repeat those to yourself every day. When you start to go down that negative side of things, catch yourself in the act and switch it up. Say them with genuine feeling and emotion; don't just read them. Get them into your very being, and soon you will start to believe them. As I said, this isn't going to happen overnight, but keep at it. I promise it will begin to change things, and you'll start to see things a little differently.

**4.** Find a mentor. I work with women every day to encourage and help lift and inspire them to do and be their best selves. Everyone needs someone. I have a few in my life, and I don't know what I would do without them. I love helping people gain confidence, harness the magnetic abilities they possess, and go all-in with their passion. Find those people in your life that can help you. You can learn more about how I work with women by checking out www.unhackable.com.

**5.** Surround yourself with positive influences. It's important to identify those negative factors in our lives that may be keeping us in a negative space. Negative friends can be the worst and feed on that negative self-talk. They can especially be toxic when you're working hard to change your thoughts and actions. You will find yourself taking one step forward and three steps back, so it's essential to surround yourself with positive people who empower you. You will begin to feel uplifted and have that desire for more personal growth. People will inspire you or drain you. You cannot expect positive changes in your life if you keep surrounding yourself with negative people.

The people you are with the most can lift you up as much as they can bring destruction. Maybe you've heard the quote by Jim Rohn, who says you're the average of the five people you spend the most time with. Have you ever noticed how hanging out with a positive, upbeat, creative person can lift your mood or how spending time with a Debbie Downer can drain you of your joy and energy?

One of the most important decisions you can make in getting where you want to go is to make sure that those closest to you are always on your side.

Take a close look at those five closest relationships, and determine whether these people are rooting for your success or keeping you complacent. If you surround yourself with people who support you, who will always have an atmosphere of positive energy and momentum, you'll be more successful.

You want to surround yourself with people who can empower you, encourage you, and elevate you. The right people will not only help you think bigger, but they can also inspire you to dream and become more creative with your ideas.

If you want to be a successful person, make a habit of hanging out with successful people. Let's say you want to improve your health. Hang out with people who are really health conscious and push themselves. If you want to be the best salesperson in the world, allow yourself to be mentored by someone you think is the greatest sales representative.

I want you to take some time and figure out ways to surround yourself with people who will help you become the best version of yourself. Here are three ideas to help you do just that: Seek out a family member or friend who will encourage and support you and help lift you toward your goals. Ask to spend more time with them, share what you're doing, and ask them for feedback. Have somebody close to you hold you accountable, check in with you, ask you how you're doing, and make sure you are taking steps all the time toward your goal.

- Find a few truth-tellers. These are people in your life who are honest and speak the truth to you. We all need that, you know. They're going to tell you those things you need to hear but that you don't always want to. I always say a truth-teller kind of just eliminates barricades. They help you get rid of anything that prevents you from performing at your best. I want you to always make sure the truth-teller is someone in your impact crew so that you know it will be coming from a good place.

- Find a mentor or coach who can help you with what you want to accomplish. Find someone who will help you every step of the way and be your biggest cheerleader and encourager. I also recommend you find a few groups on social media that you enjoy being part of. Don't spend mindless energy scrolling through social media; use it to your benefit.

Look up influencers on a topic you like and want to learn about. Follow groups of people who are all about encouraging and hanging out there if you need a boost. You're welcome to follow me on social media as well; I love to encourage people to be their best self and follow their passion.

- Get a coach. We always have to look for people who can help us accomplish what we need to do to get us where we need to go. I always recommend you find a coach who can help you. For instance, if your goal is to play tennis, your best bet is to find a tennis coach. You wouldn't ask your friend who **watches** a lot of tennis to teach you, would you? Spend a little time on this, and start the process of putting together your Impact Crew.

This is the most significant action step you can take toward your passion! You must grow your confidence and believe in yourself first before you can really dive into what you are passionate about and make a difference.

I want you to take some time and focus on this lesson. If you have to go back and reread it, do it! Take more notes; really put some time and effort into it. You need to transform your thoughts and know you're ready to move forward to make that dream of yours become a reality.

# DAY 20
## GOAL SETTING FLOW

*How we see ourselves is how we show up in the world.*

—Lisa Moser

Are you ready to continue with The S.T.A.G.E. Process? You've made it to G—**Goal Setting**. Now, this one is important because we can't just set a goal, believe we can do it, sprinkle in some great self-talk, and watch it happen. That's where a lot of people get stuck. There are people out there teaching that if you envision it, it will happen. They teach you it's simply going to come to you.

## NEWSFLASH, YOU HAVE TO DO THE WORK!

You can't just go around saying to yourself, I'm going to speak on stage at conferences all over the world. I see myself doing it, and I know I'll be amazing, and people will love me.

That's a great thing to tell yourself every day, but you've got to do the work to make that happen. So let's go back to my story about my friend who decided she could start her dog agility training class. She had to do her research and find out where she could go, the cost, the time commitment, and what she would need to take the class. She had to gather all that information.

My clients who have their sights set on getting healthy and losing weight have to do their research and find an eating plan they can stick with. They research gyms, personal trainers, exercise classes in their area, and the route they want to take.

They make the decision to let me be their truth-teller and hold them accountable. Then I challenge my clients to find people who want to take the journey with them. You see, there's a lot of information out there today with social media, friends, family, and the internet—all giving their advice and their opinions. We have to research what's best for us, then make a plan to stick with the process and set our goals.

Let's say you did vocalize to the world, "I'm going to speak on stage at conferences all over the world. I see myself doing it, and I know I'll be amazing, and people will love me."

You have to get your message nailed down, do all the homework you can about your topic, do the research, gather some statistics if there are any, figure out what stories you want to share in your talk, put together your outline and framework, and find an expert in the field you trust. This is what I mean when I say, "gather information and goal-set."

If you want to be an amazing, passionate, authentic speaker and kill it on stage, you need to take action, set the goal, and **do the work**. That is when you dive deep. Stay focused on your plan—your story and passion. Stay focused, and trust your gut. This is your story and your passion. Don't rush this part; do your homework, and start gathering information that will help you (and if speaking happens to be your goal, I can help. Check out my free resources on UnhackableForce.com).

We all get "nudges" (women's intuition, discernment, a gut feeling, or whatever you like to call it) affirming our next move, whether we're in the right place or pursuing the right goal and passion, but we often overlook them. Too often, we choose to believe what the world and others are saying.

We have to learn how to connect action with awareness.
We have to learn to "trust our G.U.T" (God's Urging To)–Daphne V. Smith

Optimize your impact! Although today's mission seems short and to the point, today is the day when you put a name to what it is you're moving toward. Speak it out and write it down; put a name to it. You've got this!

## BECOME A FORCE—DAY 20

Without pain, there is no payoff. Without struggle, there is no deep passion for your goal. So stop thinking your struggle is an enemy. Start to view it the same way that being stuck is merely a transition to your next stage.

If you feel your struggle is the enemy, you're going to focus on it in the same way if you feel you're stuck and view it as **stuck** (the 4-letter word stuck). You're going to focus and put all your energy into feeling stuck.

But if you are transitioning to the next stage of your life, it gets much more exciting to see where it's going to take you. It is the same with your struggle. If you look where your struggle may be leading you, it too can get much more exciting. Take some time and write down five reasons you're thankful for your struggle. Trust your gut and the direction you're going with this new way of thinking.

# DAY 21
## EMPOWER SELF AND QUIET THE CRITIC

*Stop letting your mind bully you. Shut it down!*

—Lisa Moser

Welcome back, you've made it to the end of The S.T.A.G.E. Process, and we're finishing up with E—**Empower!** I'll add a few more words for emphasis (hey, that starts with an "E" too!). I'll start with "**equip and execute**" because I want you to make sure you're mentally equipped to move forward and are ready to take action on what you want to do.

You have your sights set on what you're moving toward; you're working hard on transforming your thoughts and your mind into a belief system that tells you you're going to be able to do what you need to move forward. You have cleaned up the RAM on your internal computer. You've taken time to activate your passion and find your impact crew—those who will empower and be there for you and help you move toward becoming the best version of yourself. (*We would love to be a part of your Impact Crew and have you join us in the Force! Check out our website at UnhackableForce.com.)*

You've worked to gather all the information you can toward your goal, and you have equipped yourself with everything you need to move forward in this process.

Now, here's a little tip that helped me. I want you to place reminders around your home, in your car, and in your office with exactly what your intentions are. I always tell people this might feel silly or cliche, but always write down your major goal and exactly what you want to accomplish. Put it on a post-it note or a note card, and then place those strategically around your house where you're going to see them every day. Maybe put it on the bathroom mirror or the refrigerator. I have little post-it notes on my computer screen and sometimes on the dash of my car.

It serves as a constant reminder of where you're going, what your sights are set on, and that everything you're doing should be in alignment with that goal. Also, empower yourself with motivational quotes, things that speak to your heart, and place those where you'll see them as well. You always need to have positive mental notes in front of you.

Look, I know life will come at you—that's a guarantee—but it's all on how we decide to handle it. You're going to have days where you feel like what you're doing simply isn't working, or you're not producing exactly what it is you want. Know that's okay, and when it does happen, remember I told you it probably would.

You've got this because you're passionate about what you want to do, and you're moving in the right direction—the empowering notes placed strategically where you'll see them will be reminders of that. Once you have empowered yourself, you'll need to begin envisioning yourself reaching your goals. That is very important because if you can't picture yourself sharing your message with the world, writing that book, or taking a dog agility class, then it's like riding a bike with a blindfold.

You may be able to ride a bike, but if you can't see where you're going, you're probably not going far. You have a great dream, but if you can't envision yourself taking your dream to the next level, you will never get there.

Before I competed for Mrs. International, my coach was the first woman who taught me the power of our mental images. She explained to me how every morning she wanted me to envision myself standing on the stage and being announced as the winner—the new Mrs. International! That was something entirely new for me. To that point in my life, I had never been exposed to the idea of *changing my thoughts to see how things could change my world internally, and it* took some practice.

Every day I would get up and envision myself standing on the stage while the host announced the fourth runner-up, third runner-up, second runner-up, and first runner-up. Then I would picture my name somewhere in those finalist positions, and I couldn't understand why my mind stopped and put me at one of those spots.

But I kept doing the process: Fourth runner-up, third runner-up, second runner-up, Lisa Moser!

Okay, I was moving up a little bit in the right direction.

Then I remember the day I envisioned myself on stage with the host announcing the runners-up in order. She started with:

Fourth runner-up—

Third runner-up—

Second runner-up—

First runner up—

And the new Mrs. International is—*oh no, did I move myself out of the running altogether?*

Lisa Moser!

I was so ecstatic that in my mind, I had just won. I think I was almost as excited that day as I was on the actual day I won. I took my walk down that runway in my mind as a confident, passionate woman ready to take on this responsibility, and I truly felt it. I remember calling my coach up right away and yelling, "*I won! I finally won!*"

My coach knew the struggles I had with this exercise and was the one who told me to keep doing it. We celebrated together!

**Winning in your own mind, no matter what it is, is the first step into truly believing that you can do what you set your sights on.**

## BECOME A FORCE—DAY 21

It's time to execute what you are learning. You're never going to grow and get better if you don't step out of your comfort zone and start putting into practice what you are learning. So, here we go. Here's your first action item.

I want you to silence your inner critics!

"You must strive to find your own voice. Because the longer you wait to begin, the less likely you are to find it at all." — John Keating, ***Dead Poets Society***

How many of these statements have you had about yourself?

- I often get in my way.

- I am my own worst enemy.

- I am very self-critical.

- I struggle with self-limiting beliefs.

- I doubt my abilities.

- I don't see my greatness.

- I know all my weaknesses.

- I never finish anything.

- I don't want to put something out unless it's perfect.

- I am not good enough to do what I want to do.

If you're like most women, you've let one or more of these statements hack you. It's time to take hold of the positive self-talk. Stop bullying yourself! If you learn to silence the inner critic, your life will change forever!

That has been a game-changer for me. Trust me, even at my age, I fall back into this many times, but I no longer stay there. If I can't come out of it myself, my impact crew will quickly get me out of it.

My heart breaks for women I meet who are in that stuck place. They don't feel freedom in themselves and who they are, and they don't have any dreams, aspirations, or goals they want for their lives. So many of them are on autopilot or radiating so much negative energy that they can't see that everything they are going through is for a bigger purpose.

Back to my example of the goal of being a fantastic speaker and sharing your message with the world—you have to see yourself being comfortable on the stage or social media. Maybe you want to give a talk in front of thousands of people, or perhaps you want to be a YouTube sensation or move millions of people to make a positive change in their life, and you know you can help them. You have to envision yourself doing it and making it happen.

It has to start in your mind to see it vividly and know that you will get there with work. It's like injecting Setting Your Sights with steroids. I recommend that every day, you take a few minutes (I do it while I'm lying in bed) and envision yourself doing exactly what it is you want to do with your dream and your story. It is a really powerful exercise I hope you'll take the time to do.

When you change your thoughts to *I'm no longer stuck but transitioning to the next stage,* your struggle becomes your purpose. You're trusting your gut and that God-given urge to do what you're called to do. That is when your passion takes over, and you experience joy in the journey and a clear vision for where you're going. If you still need more clarity go access my FREE bonus on UnhackableForce.com.

**Write your story. What do you envision for yourself?**

# Day 22

## TAKE A BOW, THE PROCESS WORKS

*When it comes to our God-given calling,
we are SUPERNATURAL!*

—Lisa Moser

There are five steps to the S.T.A.G.E Process.

1. Set Your Sights

2. Transition Your Thoughts

3. Activate Your Passion

4. Get Into Goal Setting Flow

5. Empower Yourself and Quiet the Critic

Going through these five steps anytime you struggle to find your passion, purpose, and story and feel stuck (or transitioning, as you have learned to call it) is a game-changer. This is a great process to go through any time, and it's how we become Unhackable!

I want to share a story with you about a time I felt stuck. I knew in my heart it was a transition phase, but geez, was I in this *transition phase* for a really long time!

I had recently released my book *Miss Conception* and had been working on it for eighteen months. Now mind you, life was happening inside those eighteen months, so it wasn't all focusing on my book. My husband got a job transfer; we had to sell our home, buy a new home, transition our two boys who were then in middle school to a new school during the school year, and move farther away from our two daughters who were in college, away from our friends and family. It was a whole lot of transition during the time of writing my book.

Once I finished the book, I truly felt stuck—in a new city I didn't know, struggling with one son who didn't do well with the move, missing my friends and family, and feeling lonely. There was also a whole lot of *what the heck do I do now that my book is done?*

It's like I had a goal set to finish my book, and I knew exactly what I was working on even during all the crazy transitions with my life. Once I transitioned out of writing a book, I felt truly stuck with what was next. Working through The S.T.A.G.E Process from start to finish took a bit longer for me then.

Sometimes we take more time on certain steps, and we wonder what the heck is happening. If you do the process correctly, that is where you really dive in with your positive squad. They always knew me well and could help me see things I didn't see clearly! They helped me take all of the *Open Tabs* in my head and get them on paper.

130

They helped me figure out what I needed to do to get to the heart of my next best step. I allowed myself to walk through my pain and struggle and felt God was indeed leading me because my passion and heart were leading me. Trust me, ladies, this is where the magic happens! Once I put all the pieces together, my world opened up, and I saw a whole new path to my calling!

It got hard—really hard—and there were times I wanted to quit and told myself I was getting too old to start anything new. Thank God for my impact crew. Those people in my life saw more for me than I allowed myself to see. Surround yourself with those kinds of people and become a force with us. We would love to be some of your impact crew; we all need each other!

## BECOME A F.O.R.C.E.—DAY 22

Okay, ladies, you are rounding third base and headed to home plate! If you have followed each day and done the work, you are super excited to get started with Niccie. She is going to help you in these next seven days to step boldly into what you were called to do. Remember:

- Keep going when it gets hard.

- Find your people, and don't keep everything inside.

- Trust your gut, and know God is urging you to a bigger story.

- Know deep down what your heart is passionate about because you have lived your story.

- Be confident that you have everything it takes inside of you. When that song you haven't heard in twenty years plays, you sing like you're the rock star who wrote it.

There's something inside you that is your purpose in this beautiful thing called life! That purpose doesn't have to be some grand, elaborate goal that makes people *think* you're supernatural or something; it simply needs to get you excited to get up every day. Know that when it comes to our God-given calling—

*We are supernatural!*

# PART 4

## UNHACKABLE CALL

# DAY 23

## EMBODY YOUR DIVINE MASTERY OVER WORLDLY SLAVERY

*Do not conform to the pattern of this world, but be
transformed by the renewing of your mind. Then you will be
able to test and approve what God's will is—
is good, pleasing and perfect will.*

—Romans 12:2 (NIV)

Romans 12:2 speaks of a truth we are now beginning to prove with science. In the past, scientists thought the brain stopped developing after the first few years of life. That has been disproved through recent research regarding neuroplasticity. We now know that stroke and head injury patients can create new neural channels and regain function in ways medicine never knew. So, if we have programmed thoughts from past experiences, our upbringing, or what we have simply allowed ourselves to believe, that affects the outcomes of our lives. Why not change our thoughts and change our lives?

*Neuroplasticity is an umbrella term referring to the ability of your brain to reorganize itself, both physically and functionally, throughout your life due to your environment, behavior, thinking, and emotions. Thanks to the relatively recent capability to visually "see" into the brain allowed by functional magnetic resonance imaging (fMRI), science has confirmed this incredible morphing ability of the brain.*[18]

**We can change these thoughts, which will change our beliefs, which in turn changes our actions.** It's been proven. So, what kind of thoughts and ideas carry the power to take us farther than we ever thought possible? *Jesus looked at them and said, "With man this is impossible, but with God all things are possible."* (Matthew 19:26 NIV)

While neuroplasticity allows us to create and strengthen new neural pathways, "flow" enables us to shorten the gap to mastery (high-level functioning). Athletes have been getting into flow for years, and now they are learning to tune out distractions and zone into that flow stage faster.

What if you were able to tune out distractions, zone in on one task at hand, and accomplish what you want to or feel called to do remarkably faster and more successfully?

It wasn't until I was forty-six years old that I began to Tap into the Trinity, as I call it, my form of flow. It moved me from idea to ideation faster than anything I could have ever imagined. In one year, I went from

**May 2015:** I'm bored despite being in a job I loved, as a director of nursing, for 20+ years, to

**October 2015:** I founded my LLC, *Fulfill Your Legacy*, and got certified as a Life Coach while working.

**April 2016:** I signed a contract to write four books based on my coaching, *The Legacy Series*, a faith-based discipleship program in four parts—transforming your life, home, the community, and the nation.

Knowing how to Tap into the Trinity has kept me with God, swiftly opening doors, leading the way, and zoning in on all He has called me to be ever since.

I love helping people get into this sweet spot—that place empowered by the work you do, the health you are in, and the relationships you have. The Sweet Spot is also where you are living, loving, learning, and leading according to the calling God has for your life.

Even though at age forty-six, I was magnifying flow with the power of the Trinity, out of necessity, I actually learned how to get into flow at an early age. I struggled with a reading disorder, and I didn't know what flow was or that everyone didn't do it. Simply to read, I had to learn how to tune out the world and distractions. I found the only way to read was to read fast. I had to focus hard, read ahead, and play a game of word scramble and sentence context to get it all reworded in a way that would make sense.

Later, I realized the much-needed skill of deep concentration could be repurposed into many areas of my life.

The exciting and scary thing about our actions and thoughts being pliable is that the brain doesn't care where our thoughts originate.

**That is the most powerful part of today's training.**

Did you have or know of a child who was terrific when she was at home but as soon as she spent time with the naughty neighbor, she began to act up?

**Well, what is consuming your thoughts?**
**The naughty neighbor?**

What do you listen to on your radio, watch on your television, or look at on your cell phone? Who do you listen to or ask for advice? All of that is affecting us, whether or not we want to admit it. We become a slave to what we listen to, believe, or allow to soak into our thoughts. The definition of *slave* is "bound to obey."[19]

Our thoughts program our actions. Today's assignment will open your eyes to who and what has programmed your thoughts and, inevitably, your actions and life. It will also inspire you to take your thoughts captive. (2 Corinthians 10:5)

## BECOME A FORCE—DAY 23

Let's Embody your Mastery.

What skills would you like to acquire? If you lean into Jesus, you are no longer held back by your past. You've laid the past at the feet of the cross, so dream big.

What abilities would push you closer to the favor God has in store for you? Often, the "what" questions are more difficult than the *how* questions. I mastered business, marketing, and coaching with Deliberate Magnetic Focus, Optimal Human Performance—Focus and Flow.

That's **how** I did it, but choosing what skills to master is more complex. That is why I decided to zone in on **what** I was designed for and why I added the *Sweet Spot Assessment* early on in my coaching practice for my clients.

**We need to know how we are uniquely created and for what purpose.**

When I wasn't exactly sure of my purpose or calling, I decided to focus on the only truth I knew. I had been doing life based on what others thought of me, where I thought the world wanted me to go (patterns of the world), and I actually learned to do this world pretty well.

I loved my life until God got hold of me, making me very bored with my once well-lived life. I believe He nudged me to want more out of life and use Him to get to it. Sometimes we miss God's nudges, we feel an unsettling, maybe that we want more and don't know why. If that's you, enjoy my *'Want More Out of Life Masterclass'* and Sweet Spot Assessment found at UnhackableForce.com.

The world is doing its best right now to transform our thoughts, even telling us our personal emotions dictate actual truth, that what we identify with and believe as truth is fact. Well, understanding neuroplasticity helps you to see how the world has managed to pull that off.

If what we believe as truth comes from many outside sources, how do we ensure the world feeds us the real truth? And if one viewpoint is true, then how can we also say another perspective is also true? That is why I began tuning out the world's truth and programming my thoughts with God's truth and light. (Romans 12:2) As great as my life was, suddenly, I no longer wanted to live, dream, and do life based on lies or half-truths that the world had convinced me of.

Let's look at your current level of neuroplasticity.

**1. Have you created conditions for Divine Mastery** (In the habit of Tapping into the Trinity)?

- How is your prayer life?

- Do you ask God for direction and to hear His voice?

- Do you read the Bible?

- Do you have wise counsel, so are those you ask for insight, aside from God, Tapped into the Trinity?

- Is what you watch, listen to, and consume good for you (God-good like Christian radio, podcasts, or innocent television programming)?

2. **Have you created conditions for Worldly Slavery** (falling prey to the world, its patterns, and often addictions)?

- Do you believe what your teachers, parents, bosses, peers have said about you?

- Have you done what seemed logical?

- What consumes your idle thoughts? What do you watch on television or listen to? This is what you are programming into your life. Do you want that life?

3. **Kary talks about our behaviors becoming habits or addictions**—things we have to do each day and things we often don't even realize we are doing. Regardless, we become slaves to our thoughts. So, let's look carefully at our patterns as well as the source of our thoughts. Be honest.

- Are you addicted to anything: caffeine, alcohol, exercise, alone time, shopping, watching videos, gaming, hobbies? (Some may seem good, some not.)

- If so, what are those addictions?

- Did you leave any out? Go back to #2 and write them down.

- Do you understand that these addictions are hacking you and preventing you from reaching greater levels of Flow?

4. **Do you want to experience the positive side of neuroplasticity and rewire your brain** to achieve the life of favor God has in store for you?

**5. What new skills, habits, or abilities would you like to master?**

**6. From your list above, pick the #1 skill or ability you want next.**

In the remainder of the Flow module, we'll shorten the gap to mastery through Optimal Human Performance and, specifically, the nine Flow triggers in Day 25.

Answer yes or no to the following questions:

- I showed up filled up today and took one step closer toward becoming unhackable.

- I got hacked today, and here's how. If you got hacked, repeat the assignment until you're successful.

Day 23 of 30 is complete. I'll see you tomorrow on Day 24.

I embodied my Father's mastery. I'm one step closer to the call God has on my life and becoming an Unhackable Force!

# DAY 24
## ENGAGE YOUR GOD-GIVEN MAKE-UP

*Americans are literally killing themselves trying to achieve artificially the same sensations that flow produces naturally.*

—Steven Kotler

Let's take a look at your past. Is there anything from your past you have started and loved—as long as you were growing, building, and improving? Once your growth plateaued and things got difficult, did you back off, did it lose its luster, or did you decide it must not have been for you after all?

It's very common, but after faith-based coaching for five years, I have come to realize hard does not equal wrong. God does great work with us in those difficult times.

"Oh, God must not have wanted me to do that." We Christians can be good at pulling out this card when necessary. Thank goodness Moses led our ancestors to the promised land. Captain Sully landed on the Hudson, Flemming discovered penicillin, and Mother Theresa led an extraordinary life of service. None of them stopped when things got hard, leaving them wondering where God was and if they were doing the right things.

The moment life, goals, and dreams become too challenging, we often step away. I've felt the pain of this myself. Some turn to unhealthy patterns to push their limits. Ironically, it is at that very moment you are able to tap into a power that far exceeds any outside influence, and it is available to all of us. But very few use it.

God equipped your brain with everything you need—in this case, neurochemicals. You do not need to turn to drugs, caffeine, and dangerous means to get more than you feel capable of. You've been designed and created with everything already inside of your brain. When you get into your flow state, you have what's called a cascade of five neurochemicals:

- **Norepinephrine:** Increases heart rate, emotional control, and attention.

- **Dopamine:** Provides superhuman focus, pattern recognition, and skill-enhancing abilities.

- **Endorphins:** Augment lateral thinking.

- **Anandamide:** Provides power to link contrasting ideas together.

- **Serotonin:** Provides the ability to withstand discomfort and stay on task despite pain.

In his book, *Unhackable*, Kary Oberbrunner shares how we can become 500 percent more productive in flow.

You can perform fast and reactive with adrenaline outside of flow, but this reactive way gives you only three stressful options: fight, flight, or freeze.

It's your life and your call. You can either experience the benefits of flow the way God intended, surrendering yourself to receive in a state of stress, quit, or settle for an inferior chemical substitute that often leads to addiction.

Norepinephrine, dopamine, endorphins, anandamide, and serotonin are endogenous, meaning they originate within you naturally. The illegal drugs many people use are an irresponsible attempt to mimic a flow-like experience, and abusing these chemicals comes with severe consequences.

We have a choice to achieve a higher level of performance with grit, which has its limits, through biblical fortitude by tapping into all God has for us, or by chemically and artificially forcing our mind, body, and soul to respond. These paths have been available for centuries.

*Pharmakeia* is a Greek word used in the Bible to explain how necromancers used witchcraft and sorcery to affect the body in magical and powerful ways. These chemicals and our wrongful use of them have been plaguing us for centuries.

| Authentic | Artificial | Benefit |
|---|---|---|
| Norepinephrine | Speed | increases heart rate, emotional control, attention |
| Dopamine | Cocaine | superhuman focus, pattern recognition, skill-enhancing abilities. |
| Endorphins | Heroin Oxycotin | withstand discomfort |
| Anandamide | Marijuana | augments lateral thinking, link contrasting ideas together |
| Serotonin | Antidepressants | stay on task in spite of pain |

God made us perfectly with the natural ability to perform at levels far greater than anything we ever thought possible if we so choose.

So, let's learn more about how to step out naturally, boldly, and confidently with a God-partnered mind/body/soul experience. When we depend on synthetic drugs to produce a manufactured response, we quickly become dependent, which leads to addiction. Learning how the body works allows us to Tap into the Trinity for His super on our natural (supernatural-with God). Let's break down how they work on our mind, body, and soul.

Let's start today's homework; we will call it your micro-flow session.

## BECOME A FORCE—DAY 24

1. **Turn off all distractions.** This means all dings, beeps, buzzers—everything.

2. **Get a pair of headphones and turn up the sound** on your music of choice. Be sure it speaks nothing but life by tone and words.

3. **Prepare to be completely focused** for five minutes doing nothing else but relaxing and listening.

4. **Choose to let your mind seek:**

   a. God's insight, direction, ideas, discernment, and teaching.

   b. Let your body receive mercy, be ready for prophecy, and perceive how He calls you to shepherd.

   c. Open your heart to how He wants you to help, contribute, evangelize, and step out in blind faith.

Answer the following questions yes or no.

- I'm engaging in my God-given make-up.

- I'm one step closer to the calling God has on my life and becoming an Unhackable Force!

Day 24 of 30 is complete. I'll see you tomorrow on Day 25.

# DAY 25
## UNDERSTAND YOUR GOOD AND BAD TRIGGERS

*When you fear or resist the next move, go out boldly
with Trinity power. Surrender your pride, and take
God-partnered risks for glory-seat growth.*

—Niccie Kliegl

Because we didn't understand Flow until the last couple
of decades, we didn't know how to reproduce it in
real-time. Throughout the centuries, warriors attributed
superhuman success on the battlefield as a gift from the gods.
Writers credited breakthroughs in their books because of
visits from their muse. I wrote my last two books in a matter
of days, and I cannot take the credit. I look back at how He
has created and unfolded the most intricate series that alone
I wouldn't have been able even to dream up. That is why I
have such a passion for teaching those looking for their life
purpose and calling—to Tap into the Trinity.

Today, because of advances in neuroscience, we're more
aware of the conditions conducive for achieving a natural

Flow state. As a result, Unhackable people leverage these triggers, reverse engineer the process, and organize their lives around Flow.

I've always been a bit cautious of those overzealous with the power of self, and while learning how to get into the flow of our Father, I fear it can be a dangerous thing when left to self.

Flow will help you tune out distractions and perform better, faster, and harder. I am sure God delights in knowing we are advancing, but surely not at the cost of the cross.

*Can you imagine the Force one could catapult their calling with if they knew how to combine the Trinity with their highest functioning self? I'm passionate about helping you do this for God's glory. —Niccie Kliegl*

Kary Oberbrunner, with *Unhackable*, has identified five internal flow triggers and four external Flow triggers. Unpacking these triggers will help you understand them and, more importantly, help you organize your life around Flow. Some of these will feel familiar because we've already encountered them within the Idea and Focus modules.

## INTERNAL TRIGGERS

1. **Fully Present: Demands singularity of time and space** (no multitasking). As long as you're belaboring the past or worrying about the future, Flow will elude you. To experience Flow, you must be fully open to the present—no switch-tasking or dissociation.

2. **Defined Deadline: Output is no longer optional.** Desire without a deadline is just a wish, and a deadline isn't enough by itself. *Simply because you have a destination, doesn't mean you have motivation. Urgency is what gets you moving in full force.* Paying a penalty

for missing your deadline injects a serious dose of motivation. Be sure you get yourself into the habit, a program where you set good goals and stay growing.

3. **Authentic Ownership: Participation is mandatory, and you influence the outcome.** You have free will, so choosing not to believe in yourself or God means you've already stepped out of Flow. Most all the groups, courses, programs I start, I do to hold myself accountable, to slow down, to look back at how I was or wasn't distracted, which helped me to zone in better in the future. Doing that teaches us to live in our sweet spot, where God wants us—where blind faith becomes easier and we are more willing to go out boldly.

4. **Risk is relative, and there's a personal cost for failing.** Surgeons risk the health of their patients when they fail. I risk not communicating to my readers what God wants me to. Struggling to read as a child had its cost and benefits too. I learned early on to get used to failing in the world while working toward more. I had to be willing to risk looking dumb as I began to step into Flow. As I risked humility and focused on reading, my words pieced together, my pace evened out, and I could not only read the jigsaw puzzle with great speed, but I could also comprehend like never before! One of the most powerful blessings of this unabandoned, rightly focused risk is self-love. My stepfather taught me early that my value was never attached to my performance, just as my Heavenly Father did. *We love because he first loved us.* (1 John 4:19 NIV)

*So go out boldly, my friends. Surrender your pride and take God-partnered risks for Glory-seat Growth.*
*—Niccie Kliegl*

**5. Rich Rewards: Autotelic experiences are embedded with purpose.** Mihaly Csikszentmihalyi, the author of the book *Flow*, described internally driven people who may exhibit a sense of purpose and curiosity as autotelic. He described autotelic as "having a purpose in and not apart from itself." The word comes from the Greek αὐτοτελής, *autotelēs* (from αὐτός, autos, self, and τέλος, telos, "goal"). This self-determination is different from external drive, where things such as comfort, money, power, or fame are the motivating force. Here is where I like to remind my clients that they better get comfortable being uncomfortable.

**FLOW**

**FAVOR**

*When you are God-partnered (He is within you), He will be taking you to the next level, and with each newly mastered level, will continually raise you up higher with each action of blind God-partnered faith.*
*—Niccie Kliegl*

## EXTERNAL TRIGGERS

**1. Clear Goal: This is a big *why* combined with a big win.** Flow doesn't favor fuzziness. You know this from earlier—if you want to claim a big victory, you need to clarify a big why. John F. Kennedy's goal was clear: to land a man on the moon by the end of the decade. His speech made that abundantly clear. Rather than helping my coaching clients develop good goals, I help them hear and step into God-goals.

2. **Unpredictability: Neuroplasticity is the by-product of new pathways.** As you learn something new or engage in novel experiences, your neural circuits alter your brain. Neurons communicate with one another through particular junctions called synapses, and repeated exposure causes these specific circuits to fire again and again. The stronger these synaptic connections become, the more your brain is rewired. Neurons that fire together wire together.

   Neuroplasticity is neutral, meaning it can work for you or against you. It can create conditions for slavery or mastery, depending on the context. I saw too many people building negative destinies, then wondering why their lives were so difficult and where God was. I created a coaching tool called *Cognitive Awareness—Putting on New Self* to help my clients steer clear of bad programming and instead turn to the Trinity to transform the mind. (You can access the form at UnhackableForce.com in the I want more out of life free resourse.)

*Put off your old self, which belongs to your former manner of life and is corrupt through deceitful desires, and to be renewed in the spirit of your minds, and to put on the new self, created after the likeness of God in true righteousness and holiness.* Ephesians 4:22–23

3. **Feedback Loops: Truth-Tellers' Fast-track Flow.** In some ways, Flow is a team effort. Of course, you're the sole benefactor of the neurochemicals racing through your brain. However, to experience and

sustain Flow, you often need feedback loops that provide data and allow you to course correct.

*This is why regularly meeting together is a key part of our faith. 25 not giving up meeting together, as some are in the habit of doing, but encouraging one another—and all the more as you see the Day approaching.* (Hebrews 10:25 NIV)

I encourage you to get into a great church and find a God-partnered community like the Legacy Leaders and Unhackable Force. We know the power of feedback; God has written it into our days from the beginning of time with the Sabbath for self-reflection.

But it gets better; if we have truth-tellers who also tap into the truth, we can step into our calling more quickly by disregarding what affects us poorly and embracing God's glory with blind faith action Truth-Tellers Fast-track Flow.

## 4. Challenge to Competence Ratio: A perfect blend means you'll be perfectly present.

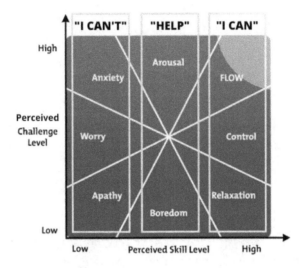

Notice the chart. It's all about perception. On the left side, you'll see perceived challenges. If the challenge is high and your skills are too low, you feel anxious, but if your skills are high and the challenge is too low, you're bored. You want what's called the "Flow channel." It's the perfect blend of stretch without snap. That is how I learned to read and got into Flow for the following years.

Look at the right side of the table. By learning to relax (surrender) into my new self and take control with my God-partnered thoughts (truth and light), I could have a perceived low skill level but perform on the I can side reaching Flow fast. I absolutely love helping others be authentic with where they are on this graph and showing them how to get into Flow for their desired God-partnered skill.

# BECOME A FORCE—DAY 25

## TAKE THE FLOW TRIGGER ASSESSMENT

- **The Deep—I only focus on one task at a time.**

Never (1) Almost Never (2) Often (3) Almost Always (4) Always (5)

- **Defined Deadline—I have clearly defined deadlines.**

Never (1) Almost Never (2) Often (3) Almost Always (4) Always (5)

- **Authentic Ownership—My life requires me to show up filled up, and I know I influence the outcome.**

Never (1) Almost Never (2) Often (3) Almost Always (4) Always (5)

- **Real Risk—With my commitments, I have a real personal cost for failing.**

Never (1) Almost Never (2) Often (3) Almost Always (4) Always (5)

- **Rich Rewards—I experience Flow states integrated with Boon achievement.**

Never (1) Almost Never (2) Often (3) Almost Always (4) Always (5)

- **Clear Goal—I have a big why combined with a big win.**

Never (1) Almost Never (2) Often (3) Almost Always (4) Always (5)

- **Unpredictability—My brain experiences large amounts of neuroplasticity.**

Never (1) Almost Never (2) Often (3) Almost Always (4) Always (5)

- **Feedback Loops—I have Truth-Tellers and data to help me fast-track Flow.**

Never (1) Almost Never (2) Often (3) Almost Always (4) Always (5)

- **Challenge to Competence Ratio—My life is a perfect blend of high challenge and high skills.**

Never (1) Almost Never (2) Often (3) Almost Always (4) Always (5)

Answer the following questions yes or no.

- I showed up filled up today.
- I'm one step closer to the calling God has on my life and becoming an Unhackable Force!

Day 25 of 30 is complete. I'll see you tomorrow on Day 26.

# DAY 26
## ASSESS YOUR GROWTH FOR
## SABBATH-STYLE EXCELLENCE

*Look back each week and assess all the good that you and
God did. If you find areas in need of excellence, invite God
back into them for a brighter and more powerful tomorrow.*

—Niccie Kliegl

You'll soon share your favor with yourself and your
world, in that order. For many people, this is the first
time they'll truly give themselves permission to own
yesterday, but then, more importantly, dream freely without
judgment or restraint for tomorrow.

This work might feel odd as well, realizing you can run—
yes, I mean RUN—into God's favor for your life, freely,
without borders, barriers, or boundaries. He will be guiding
and directing you. Go boldly with Him. Even the enemy will
not be able to bring down your calling and favor.

*You intended to harm me, but God intended it for good to
accomplish what is now being done, the saving of many lives.*
(Genesis 50:20 NIV)

*Examine yourselves to see whether you are in the faith; test yourselves. Do you not realize that Christ Jesus is in you—unless, of course, you fail the test?* (2 Corinthians 13:5 NIV)

Write your findings and see them. Were you alone, protected, guided? Did you step out in blind faith, and was it filled with favor? Give yourself the gift of assessing your growth. Be pleased with how far you've come rather than how far you have left to go. Dan Sullivan advises people to measure the gain, not the gap. Think of this like the Sabbath. Consider all the work God knew was coming, yet he took the time to sit back on day seven to assess his work and to say, "It is good."

## BECOMING A FORCE—DAY 26

Take the Unhackable F.O.R.C.E. Assessment now, and fill in your score for both Day 1 and today.[20]

# UNHACKABLE
## ASSESSMENT

| CATEGORY | DAY 1 | DAY 26 |
|----------|-------|--------|
| IDEA | | |
| FOCUS | | |
| FLOW | | |
| RESULT | | |

Now answer the following questions to help you clarify the progress you have made, if you did it alone, or if you had help. That will reinforce how to get back into Flow in the future.

1. What are your feelings about the two different assessment results?

_____

_____

2. Do you believe you've grown these past twenty-five days? If so, how?

_____

_____

3. What is your biggest takeaway from the book so far?

_____

_____

4. In big or small ways, how has your thinking changed?

_____

_____

The Unhackable women love to share each other's wins! Please take a picture of yourself and post your score along with one new idea that has begun to unfold.

It might seem so far off, or it might have already come to fruition. We simply want to train you to tap into God's great power, turn away from the noise of the world, listen for answers and direction, respond fearlessly with blind faith, and then give God the Glory while you also celebrate your wins!

# DAY 27
## CLARIFY YOUR CALL THROUGH WISDOM OVER KNOWLEDGE

*The point is that these things we know don't qualify as wisdom unless we actually practice them. Maybe true wisdom is simply acting consistently on what we already know to be true, honorable, just, pure, lovely, commendable, excellent, or praiseworthy.*

—Greg Paul

Welcome to the final part of becoming an Unhackable Force—the Favor Ceremony. Let's finish strong. In this last part of the book, we will first (on Day 27) recap your findings for clarity, then develop your craft (Day 28) by taking action. Communicating your call (Day 29) will truly activate your Trinity power, and in our final chapter, all four of the authors will unite with you!

Today could be your most challenging day. It's going to require you to be mentally strong and show up filled up. These final days are where our callings are won and lost. Here we will learn just how much closer you are to living out your divine calling and stepping into a life of favor.

Before going forward, we need to step back. Too many times, in our Western mindset, we assume that since we've heard something, we know it or have even mastered it. Notice the difference between the Hebrew perspective of knowing and the Greek perspective.

"I already know that."
Greek *know*—I *heard* that.
Hebrew *know*—I *live* that.

*Until we can look at our life and see evidence that we've mastered unhackability, it's wise to go back and go deeper.*

## TIME TO GO EVEN DEEPER

Today, we will clarify our calling by taking action and going deeper.

**On Day 4, you picked one thing you desired to rewrite, redo, and reclaim.** We remind you that nobody sees her story, dream, and favor perfectly in the beginning. Clarity comes as you take action. Realize it is like emerging out of a fog. Embrace the paradox; the clouds lift when you move toward your desire.

Rewrite the desire you wrote that day:

**On Day 5, you counted your cost.** We told you to be honest. What fears do you have about truly committing to rewriting your story?

Rewrite the fears you had on that day:

Do those fears still scare you today? Why or why not? Write your feelings below.

**On Day 6, you claimed your promise.** We taught you that wanting to claim a big win means you need to clarify a big *why*. It isn't uncommon to want to give up along the way of brokenness. If the dream is leaning on you, understand *your idea was given through you and not to you. Then you understand it's on God to open up the heavens and pour down the promises. Your job is to believe in yourself.*

Rewrite the way you wrote through your brokenness:

**On Day 10, you created your idea.** We said the right step is always the one that requires action. Most people don't like that answer. They want clarity *before* they take action, but clarity only comes *because* we take action. The way forward is never smooth, clear, or evident in the beginning.

You did your best to Clear YOUR C.R.A.P. Rewrite it again.

**On Day 11, you committed to taking control of your time.** We said that matter could exist in two places at once. An idea manifests in the mind of a person imagining the thought and the same concept exists somewhere else in the universe simultaneously.

You choose your date to take back control of your time. Fill out that commitment in the form of a check to yourself. Endorse your check and keep it in your possession until that date.

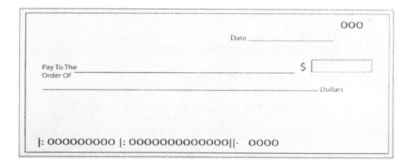

**On Day 13, you established your deadline.** We said picking a deadline is essential. It's similar to choosing a destination for a road trip. Without one, you're going in circles, but a deadline isn't enough simply because you have a *destination*. A goal also doesn't mean you have motivation. What gets you moving in full force is urgency. Paying a penalty for missing your deadline injects a severe dose of inspiration. You defined your destination, motivation, and deadline. Rewrite it again.

**On Day 21, you silenced your self-critic.** I said if you were like most people, you've left yourself for one or more of these statements that hacked you:

- I often get in my own way.

- I am my own worst enemy.

- I am self-critical.

- I struggle with self-limiting beliefs.

- I doubt my abilities.

- I don't see my greatness.

- I know all my weaknesses.

- It is tough for me to identify my strengths.

- I never finish anything.

- I don't want to put something out unless it's perfect.

You discovered it was time to get out of your own way and get into Flow. Rewrite the life of favor you envision again.

## BECOMING A FORCE—DAY 27

### CLARIFY HOW YOUR LIFE IS RESET, REDONE, AND RECLAIMED

Based on this recap, look how far you've come. You know much more today than when you first started because you took action.

"Keep in mind, clarity is a tricky thing most people naïvely say they want without understanding that clarity comes with a cost. That's the danger with clarity; once you know what you want, you're dissatisfied with anything less."[21]

This step is the point of no return. The growing clarity you've been experiencing will lead you through a series of other steps explained in the book *The Deeper Path* (which is part of each author's private coaching and our workshops). We called the process below The Deeper Path payoff. Notice that you begin with clarity and conclude with income. That income may be measured in monetary, relational, spiritual, physical, or emotional wealth.

## THE DEEPER PATH PAYOFF

Are you ready for more? Having completed your favor recap, you now take time to clarify your call. Don't aim for perfection, and remember what Steve Jobs said: *"You can only connect the dots looking backward."*

I encourage you to get in a quiet place and create a space conducive to deep thinking. Play some clarifying music if it helps. Listen to that music for at least a minute with your eyes closed before writing.

What new insights and awareness do you have about your life of favor?

_____

_____

_____

_____

_____

_____

# DAY 28

## CRAFT YOUR FAVOR STATEMENT
## WITH GOD'S SCRIPT

*There are times to stick to the script. This is not one of them.
Your Boon is intended to disrupt—all Flawless Ideas do.*

—Kary Oberbrunner

Today I will start the chapter off-script. We will turn to the Word as we prepare to move forward in our call and the favor we long for. We have done the work, we are getting clear, and now the world will do its best to keep us from uniting and tapping into all the power that awaits us and becoming the fierce women we are called to be.

Look at the text below and note how God is calling us.

### LIVE UP TO YOUR CALLING!

*So, then, this is my appeal to you—yes, it's me, the prisoner in the Lord! You must live up to the calling you received. **Bear with one another in love**; be humble, meek, and patient in every* *way with one another.* **Make every effort to guard the unity** *the Spirit gives, with your lives bound together in peace.*

**There is one body and one spirit; you were, after all,** **called to one hope which goes with your call. There is one** **Lord, one faith, one baptism; one God and father of all,** **who is over all, through all, and in all.**

But **grace was given to each one of us,** *according to the measure the king used when he was distributing gifts. That's why it says*

> *When he went up on high*
> *he led bondage itself into bondage*
> *and he gave gifts to people.*

*When it says here that "he went up," what that means is that he also came down into the lower place, that is, the earth.*

*The one who came down is the one who also "went up"— yes, above all the heavens!—***so that he might fill all things***. (Ephesians 4:1 - 10 NTE)

It is by Him, through Him, and in Him that we are able to tap into all His greatness, to use our gifts fully and reap the reward fully.

The verse above is a witness to the Unhackable Force of women who bind together and unify with Him. Alone we are fierce, but together we become a force. This bond allows us to go off our script and step into our God-given favored script with confidence.

The world teaches us to stay on script, to do what they tell us, what we feel safe doing—nothing risky. After all, what would others think? We need to look back at how God has led us thus far to feel more confident moving forward.

*Was it by doing things on script that we had the most favor, or was it when we went off script, stepping and leaning into His script over ours or the world's?* Here is a highlight of how I went off my script to partner up with God. Man, did He move me more fiercely once I aligned!

- I was told that I would never read well, yet, I forged forward *knowing* it was right.

- I wasn't hired at age sixteen no matter where I applied, likely because my application looked like a fifth-grader had filled it out. Yet, I *followed God's nudge* to check the nursing home, where they hired me without an application, interviewing me and hiring me on the spot.

- I was told to become a hairdresser, so I wouldn't have to struggle through school, yet I'd *learned to accept the pain for the glory,* so I went where my heart was— to nursing school.

- I told myself at age forty-six that I should be content with my twenty-plus-year job as a director of nursing. I earned great pay, loved all my staff, patients, and families, but I followed God's nudge for more, unsure of what was to come and went out in blind faith. Now I run a hugely successful practice for the kingdom.

**This daily mission is your moment of truth.** You'll always have naysayers and doubters trying to make you stick to the script. Sometimes your strongest resistance comes from your own lips or the lips of loved ones. They mean well; they don't want to see you get hurt, and they want you to be safe and do the right thing. But sometimes, the right thing is to go off-script.

# BECOMING A FORCE—DAY 28

It's your life, and it's your choice. You are an amazing woman. Women are blessed to be creators in the most powerful way—creating a child in our very womb. Today, as you craft your Favor, you'll have to decide which script to write—the one you are all too familiar and comfortable with or the one you know you *need* to write. Write the script that God breathed into you from before your first breath.

Think of it as a "boon" speech or your rewritten God-partnered call and story that you'll share with the world. The truth is, you may share it sooner than you think. (Keep it to five minutes or less.) Speak forth your rewritten story.

Referencing Sam Phillip's exhortation to get you started:

> *If you was hit by a truck and you were lying out in that gutter dying…and you had time to give one Boon Speech, huh, one speech…people would remember before you're dirt…one speech that would let God know what you felt about your time here on earth…one speech that would sum you up. Would you say something different? Something real, something you felt? Because I'm telling you right now…that's the kind of Boon Speech people want to hear. One that changes lives.*
> —*Walk the Line* (2005) Dallas Roberts: Sam Phillips

# MY REWRITTEN STORY

# DAY 29

## COMMUNICATE YOUR FAVOR TO GAIN FAITH AND FAVOR

*Live every day like it's your last because someday, you're going to be right.*

—Muhammad Ali

I t's time to communicate your rewritten story to the Unhackable Force community. It may be unpolished and imperfect, but that's what we're looking for. The key is to take imperfect action.

- Make the most of today. See Ephesians 5:15.

- Seize the Day. (*Dead Poets Society*, Roman poet Horace's Odes, 23 BC)

### SIX SCRIPTURES ABOUT SPEAKING THINGS INTO EXISTENCE

1. *The tongue has the power of life and death, and those who love it will eat its fruit.* (Proverbs 18:21 NIV)

2. *Finally, brothers and sisters, whatever is true, whatever is noble, whatever is right, whatever is pure, whatever is lovely, whatever is admirable—if anything is excellent or praiseworthy—think about such things.* (Philippians 4:8 NIV)

3. *"If you believe, you will receive whatever you ask for in prayer."* (Matthew 21:22 NIV)

4. *So is my word that goes out from my mouth: It will not return to me empty, but will accomplish what I desire and achieve the purpose for which I sent it.* (Isaiah 55:11 NIV)

5. *Truly I tell you, if anyone says to this mountain, 'Go, throw yourself into the sea,' and does not doubt in their heart but believes that what they say will happen, it will be done for them.* (Mark 11:23 NIV)

6. *Jesus answered, "It is written: 'Man shall not live on bread alone, but on every word that comes from the mouth of God."* (Matthew 4:4 NIV)

## BECOMING A FORCE—DAY 29

Today, record yourself giving your voice to your Rewritten Story. You can do this easily on your smartphone. After recording, go to the Unhackable Force community (the Tribe). Make a post by selecting the camera icon and choosing the video you just recorded. Label it "My Rewritten Story." When you post it on the Tribe page, people outside the tribe won't be able to view it or comment on it.

Ready or not, it's your moment of truth.

Give your speech.

Record your speech.

Post your speech.

Don't believe what you *think*; Believe what you know. Today, write down what you believe you need to do to step into your call and life of favor. **Out of theory and into actuality!** It doesn't matter what you are doing—going on a vacation, taking a new job, or writing a book. Write down what you believe you need to step into your call and life of favor.

Leading into Day 30, let's prepare you for stepping in and taking action on how God uniquely made you and how He is calling you!

- Have you begun to Reset your patterns for high-achieving success in all areas of your life?

- Have you decided to REDO the dreams God planted in you before your first breath?

- Are you ready to RECLAIM your life of favor by crafting and creating?

# PART 5

## UNHACKABLE
## ELEVATION

# DAY 30
## YOUR NEXT STEPS

*When you focus on your greatness, you
elevate everyone around you.*

—Gabrielle Bernstein

## WELCOME TO THE FORCE!

We applaud the time, emotion, effort, and determination you have put into rewriting your story. Thirty days is enough time to plant deep seeds that will bring lasting results for years to come if watered.

## A NOTE FROM DEBRA—

I'd love to reach out and give you a hug right now. You have taken one of the most significant steps that only a small percentage of ladies have the courage to take.

The four stages we discussed in our section of Unhackable Favor can be applied throughout our lives. My speaking and coaching have brought consistent feedback about being A.B.L.E. Whether you are facing grief or anything life-altering, apply the same metamorphic steps, and you will work through the change with clarity.

- A: Awareness—Remember, your awareness becomes keen. Much as the caterpillar crawls and outgrows its skin several times, you will find your understanding takes on a whole new vision. You will know precisely what needs changing and attention in your life.

- B: Brokenness—Your transformation will begin with your brokenness. The lasting changes you are looking for can only take place alone in the dark. Stay with the brokenness until you see the blessing.

- L: Leverage—You must emerge slowly. The "ta-da" moment of transformation does not exist.

- E: Expectations—Girlfriend, there is no limit to your dreams. I want you to imagine yourself free and beautiful because, in reality, it is not a dream at all. You are a princess. You are a child of a King who is always there with Favor to show you a life you never dreamed of.

## A NOTE FROM DAPHNE—

Well done, Sister Friend.

Thirty days ago, you started with a decision and followed through with action and sacrifice. So what comes next? It's time to cement your growth. The permission you gave yourself to start and make changes is the same permission you need to continue. I often refer to it as it's time to Clear YOUR C.R.A.P.

That's right, I said it. Or rather, I typed it. The best way to maintain your progress is to ensure you've removed the roots of what's been keeping you in a holding pattern, back-sliding, confused, or in general, going around in circles. Here are a few quick tactics you can use to maintain what you've gained and continue your momentum.

- **C**haos: Eliminate or minimize it.

  o Wishful thinking? Not when you permit yourself to say "no," and when you take ownership of your calendar and technology tools.

- **R**ules: You are the boss of you.

  o Tap into your inner rebel and give yourself permission to break rules that no longer serve you and establish new ones that do. Simply because something has always "been done that way" does not mean it has to continue.

- **A**ttitudes: You are responsible only for yours.

  o Since this is one of the few things we truly have control over in life, choose wisely. Remember, attitudes are contagious. Whose have you caught? What if someone caught yours?

- **P**erspectives: Things in the mirror may appear larger.

  o Our viewpoint is something we get to own, and the way we perceive things is not the way someone else does or will. For that matter, are you sure yours is accurate? Check yourself before you wreck yourself.

Remember, you've already come so far; why not keep going? In this life, others will disappoint you; it's going to happen, and you can't control it. However, you can promise not to disappoint yourself. Grow on!

## A NOTE FROM LISA—

Day 30! I couldn't be more excited for you all than I am right now! You have pushed through and are ready to become a Force!

You have **S**et your sights, **T**ransformed your thoughts, **A**ctivated your passion, gotten into that **G**oal setting Flow, and you are **E**mpowered and have quieted your inner critic! You can take a bow because this process works, and you are ready to take your next **S.T.A.G.E.**!

I have one last action step I want you to take, and I hope you are ready for it! I want you to find your favorite dance song and crank that baby up! Do it right now if you can, and dance your little heart out with enthusiasm and excitement! You are on your way, my friend!

My favorite song to help me get pumped up is "Everybody Dance Now" by C+C Music Factory. Every time I hear that song, it fires me up, and I dance like nobody's watching! Yes, it's an oldie, but no matter your age, you're going to want to dance! If you prefer Christian music, I love the song "Happy Dance" by MercyMe.

*Come on, ladies, have some fun, and celebrate yourself! I'm dancing right now in my seat as I write this because I'm so excited for you all.*

## A NOTE FROM NICCIE—

I'm curious which of the thirty days helped move you closer to your calling? Which days stood out to you or caused you to pivot? I believe that the Holy Spirit was working in you, and those are the days you should lean into. *Head to UnhackableForce.com for ways to stay connected, bring us to your city, or even jump into our online workshops, studies, and retreats.*

Regardless of whether you reach out for more from our *Unhackable Force* resources, I want you to know there is always M.O.R.E. waiting for you and the calling God has for your life.

- **M: Mastery and Makeup**

  o Embody Your Divine Mastery Over Worldly Slavery.

  o Stick close to the written word through praise music, podcasts, sermons, and wise counsel.

  o Engage Your God-given Make-up.

  o Continue to learn of and advance your unique gifts and talents.

- **O: Open eyes to good triggers and Observe past greatness.**

  o Understand Your Good and Bad Triggers.

  o Pay attention to what throws you off course; that is the enemy trying to prevent you from living your calling.

  o Pay attention to doors that quickly open and bless; that is the Holy Spirit nudging you forward.

  o Assess Your Growth For Sabbath-style Excellence.

  o Remember to look back. It dramatically increases your faith as you see how God is and has worked in you. It inspires you to go out more often and be bolder.

- **R: Radiate wisdom**

  o Clarify Your Call Through Wisdom Over Knowledge: That means moving. We can learn all about the goodness of God or the great calling He has for our life, but if we never act on it, we leave our calling at the door.

  o Knowledge becomes wisdom when acted upon.

- **E: Express your favor/Elevate your faith**

    o Craft Your Favor Statement With God's Script. We need to speak it as God did. He spoke things into existence. Get those affirmations going, and be sure they are chock full of God's truths.

    o Communicate Your Favor to Gain Faith and Favor: Start sharing yourself and your calling with the world. Tell how God is nudging you. He will be using others to help you and elevate you, so start by telling yourself and others exactly what God is calling you to do.

God is calling you to more, and after completing the *Unhackable Force,* you have now learned how to Reset, Redo, and Reclaim a life of favor!

# ENDNOTES

1   Kary Oberbrunner, *Unhackable* (Powell, OH: Author Academy Elite, 2020), p. 5.

2   Oberbrunner, *Unhackable*, pp. 14-15.

3   Oberbrunner, *Unhackable*, p. 26.

4   Oberbrunner, *Unhackable*, p. 6.

5   Gary Coxe, *How To Make Your Thoughts Disappear*, p, 5.

6   Coxe, *How To Make Your Thoughts Disappear, pp. 18-19.*

7   *Oberbrunner, Unhackable*, p. 39.

8   Plumb, *Exhale* (Word Records and Curb Records, 2015)

9   Wikipedia, https://en.wikipedia.org/wiki/Metamorphosis

10  https://www.lexico.com/en/definition/metamorphosis

11  https://sciencing.com/things-go-through-metamorphosis-8140222.html

12  Dr Caroline Leaf. https://www.pinterest.com/pin/120471358759 469537/

13  https://sciencing.com/things-go-through-metamorphosis-8140222.html

14  Oberbrunner, *Unhackable*, pp. 52, 60.

15  Oberbrunner, *Unhackable*, p. 63.

16  https://iep.utm.edu/epistemo/

17  https://www.biblestudytools.com/dictionaries/bakers-evangelical-dictionary/know-knowledge.html

18  Neuroplasticity: The 10 Fundamentals Of Rewiring Your Brain by Debbie Hampton

19  https://www.lexico.com/en/definition/slave

20  (Head to unhackableforce.com/ to take assessment.)

21  Oberbrunner, *Unhackable*, p. 233.

# Welcome to the

UNHACKABLE *Force*

Join us on the journey

www.facebook.com/groups/unhackableforce

For over forty years, Debra has helped people identify areas in their life where they are stuck and need clarity by focusing on problematic issues while finding solutions to move forward.

Debra has experienced the loss of four children, abortion and its crippling aftermath, loss of both parents, divorce, and financial ruin. For years, she struggled behind a mask of pretending and performing. Debra later discovered how to remove that mask and RISE above the circumstances of life without letting them define her. Through her books, speaking, workshops, and courses, she will lead you in **Unmasking the Hope inside and Embracing a joyful Life.**

You can find out more and connect to Debra at www.Debra.Life, or simply email her: Debra@Debra.Life.

She grew up in the Smoky Mountains and currently resides in Florida with her Amazon parrot, Jazz. Debra is a very avid tennis player and enjoys all outdoor activities. She has lived in numerous places and has a deep appreciation of different cultures.

**Daphne V. Smith**, author of *What's YOUR Scarlet Letter*, coach, Daphne V TV host, and speaker, is driven to lead and encourage women to allow their hearts to heal and love themselves as Christ does.

Decades of dysfunction and abuse took their toll on

her until Daphne landed in recovery, and she began to heal. Discovering her worth and value led her on a path that would restore the lost years and clear the way for a new foundation anchored in faith and facts. Because of her transformation, she feels compelled to share hope with others.

She realized that until you Clear YOUR C.R.A.P.©, old patterns and habits are destined to repeat themselves. "We have to remove the root to experience lasting systemic transformation." Whether her clients are ready to author their life, book, or business, Daphne guides them to break their chains of lies and limiting beliefs to make waves that create the life and achieve the purpose for which they are created.

You can find out more about Daphne at DaphneVSmith.com.

She is the proud mom of two adult children and one amazing daughter-in-love. Living in the beauty and sanctuary of Northwest Arkansas near family and friends, this Texas roots girl seeks the beauty, joy, and healing every day has to offer.

**Lisa Moser** is an author, coach, and speaker who loves educating and encouraging others to understand and break free from the misconceptions that hold them hostage and keep them from finding their passion and step on to that next stage in life.

Pageantry helped her discover the value of her voice, her passion and message, and how sharing it with the world can have a huge impact. She competed in the Miss USA pageant and spent her year educating on the importance of living a well-balanced, healthy lifestyle. She later returned to pageantry and won the title of Mrs. International and used her voice and passion to raise awareness for the American Diabetes Association.

Lisa knew then that the pageant wins were for a much bigger reason than just a crown and banner. She knew that what she had learned about sharing one's voice and its impact on people was something she needed to teach others. *"We all have a gift that is meant to be shared with the world."*

You can find out more about Lisa at LisaMoser.com.

Lisa is from the great state of Ohio and has been married to her husband Don for over thirty years. They have four amazing children, a fantastic son-in-law, a granddaughter, Olive, and they love spending time with friends and family. They are big sports fans (well, minus one daughter) and Ohio State Buckeyes!! O-H!! (Those of you who are fans know what to yell back!!)

 **Niccie Kliegl**, author of *the Legacy Series*, coach, talk show host, and speaker, is passionate about elevating others into their "Sweet Spot."

She founded Fulfill Your Legacy, her life and business coaching practice, in 2015 with a faith-based discipleship program that raises up Christian leaders who first get themselves partnered with God, then bring God into their home, community, and nation. Niccie says, "Elevating others into their Sweet Spot where they get more out of life and work because they partner with God, know their divine purpose, and **Tap into the Trinity**©, is what I'm meant to do!"

Niccie is most joyful over her **Legacy Leader private community** of individuals learning to *live, love, learn,* **and** *lead* **according to the call God has on their life.** A big part of that is teaching other faith-based entrepreneurs to start their own successful online business they have been called to.

You can find out more about Niccie at NiccieKliegl.com.

She lives in Iowa and is married to her best friend and lover, Jeff Kliegl, of thirty years with two beautiful grown daughters, Raya and Riley, and grandchild, sweet Iris.

# DEBRA.LIFE

## DON'T LET A MOMENT BECOME A MINDSET

| SPEAKING | WORKSHOPS | BOOKS |
|:---:|:---:|:---:|

DEBRA@DEBRA.LIFE

# CLEAR YOUR C.R.A.P.
## LIVE BY DESIGN INSTEAD OF DEFAULT

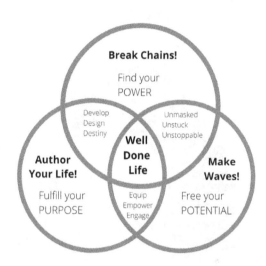

**Break Chains!**

Find your POWER

Develop
Design
Destiny

Unmasked
Unstuck
Unstoppable

**Well Done Life**

**Author Your Life!**

**Make Waves!**

Fulfill your PURPOSE

Equip
Empower
Engage

Free your POTENTIAL

## AUTHOR YOUR LIFE, BOOK, OR BUSINESS

**ONLINE TEACHING**      **SPEAKING**      **1-ON-1 COACHING**

DAPHNEVSMITH.COM

# CONNECT *for* IMPACT

## WITH LISA MOSER

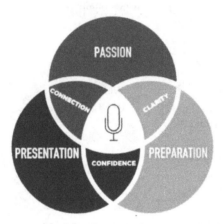

**CONNECTION IS THE KEY FOR IMPACTFUL COMMUNICATION**

COACHING          IMPACT MASTERMIND          SPEAKING

LISAMOSER.COM

# LEGACY SERIES
## WITH NICCIE KLIEGL

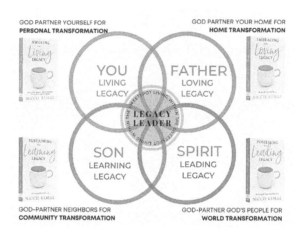

GOD PARTNER YOURSELF FOR
**PERSONAL TRANSFORMATION**

GOD PARTNER YOUR HOME FOR
**HOME TRANSFORMATION**

**YOU** LIVING LEGACY

**FATHER** LOVING LEGACY

**LEGACY LEADER**

**SON** LEARNING LEGACY

**SPIRIT** LEADING LEGACY

GOD-PARTNER NEIGHBORS FOR
**COMMUNITY TRANSFORMATION**

GOD-PARTNER GOD'S PEOPLE FOR
**WORLD TRANSFORMATION**

| SPEAKER | COACH | SUBSCRIPTION COMMUNITY |
|---------|-------|------------------------|

START YOUR LIFE/HOME/COMMUNITY/NATION TRANSFORMATION TODAY

NICCIEKLIEGL.COM

CPSIA information can be obtained
at www.ICGtesting.com
Printed in the USA
LVHW041320310822
727261LV00010B/626